It's Your Dream, Make it as Big as You Want

Riding The Great Divide Mountain Bike Route

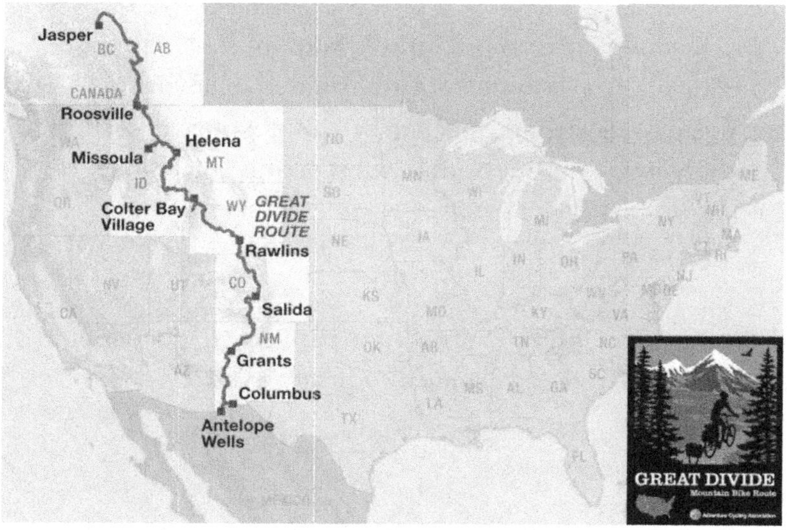

Map Courtesy of Adventure Cycling Association.

Note: The Adventure Cycling Association created and mapped the Great Divide Mountain Bike Route.

IT'S YOUR DREAM, MAKE IT AS BIG AS YOU WANT

First Edition

ISBN 13: 979-8-234-03336-9

Library of Congress Control Number: 2026907400

This is a work of nonfiction. Some names and identifying details may have been changed to protect privacy.

Published by: It's Your Dream Press
Printed in the United States of America

Cover design: Jenny Cusick / Nick Mason
Author photograph by: Jenny Cusick
Photos: Jenny Cusick/Tara Kaplan/Larry Kaplan

For those who dare to chase their dreams, and especially those who support them.

This book is dedicated to all my travel companions, and to the family and friends whose support is beyond all measure.

Contents

Preface

"Good things don't happen by themselves and rarely come when one only waits and hopes. If it is important, it is up to you to help it along, actively pursue it. When you take initiative, take that first step, you gather your energy and turn it toward your goal, bringing it closer, making it clearer. New ideas, wondrous dreams, unvoiced hopes come to life with initiative. And in making a start you gain momentum and newfound strength." -Author Unknown

This quote hung above my desk for over 30 years, while I took small steps to follow my dreams. Good things do not arrive by accident, nor do meaningful outcomes emerge from passive hope alone. Progress begins when intention is matched with action, when we decide that what matters deserves our effort.

This book is rooted in that belief: Initiative is the spark that transforms possibility into reality. Every meaningful change begins with a first step, however small, taken with purpose and resolve. The pages that follow are an invitation to move forward, to act with intention, cultivate momentum, and discover the strength that emerges only after you begin.

Chapter 1: The start of living my dreams

Liberation

I come from a generation deeply committed to one's employer. Born in 1965, just past the Baby Boomer years, I never quite identified with Generation X. Instead, I seem to belong to the micro-generation that believed work would love us back if we just tried hard enough.

Work was my priority throughout my various careers, regretfully, often above my husband and my family. I was fully engaged: long hours, enthusiastic volunteering, and a near-reflexive willingness to lead social activities. I loved working. If there was a committee, I was on it. If there was a signup sheet, my name appeared early and often. I sought the next promotion, the increased workload, the responsibility.

And yet, work was often a letdown, less fulfilling than promised, more draining than rewarding. It quietly crowded out the life I thought I would get to later. Although I vacationed the maximum time allowed, I postponed my dreams of extended adventures: bicycle touring, long backpacking trips, European rail journeys. I told myself there would be time. There always is, until there isn't.

I've read all the happiness books, the self-help books, the "how to be most efficient" books, the business management and personal management books. I recall one that indicated that $70K of annual income was the magic threshold, above which increased happiness, based on self-assessments, was not achieved. Once we had a roof over our heads, food on our plates, and a few close friendships, those who earned $70K annually were as happy as those who were very wealthy.

I wondered what "enough" meant for me now, stripped of titles and paychecks. Mom and Dad had stocked our freezer with whoopie pies and pie crusts after hearing I'd quit my job. Was that enough?

I was afraid—afraid to step away from the dependable structure of work, the steady income; afraid to admit I wanted something else;

afraid that choosing a career unrelated to engineering or management might look irresponsible or, worse, self-indulgent.

Now, I am ready to embrace my adventurous dreams. Ready, before my body fails me. Ready, though not without trepidation. Ready, with a mix of excitement and the faint angst of someone who has spent decades being dependable and is now considering becoming interesting, or boringly self-absorbed. I'm still nervous. I still hesitate. But the pull of the adventurous life I want feels stronger than the comfort of the life I know. I did it—I made the most difficult move and quit full-time employment. I quit the career track.

To be yourself in a world that kept asking for a different version. To stand beside people who know you and stay. To shape a life that fits, not one that impresses. These are the quiet freedoms I spent years postponing. Now they feel like the beginning of something honest. That, I'm learning, is the real adventure, and I'm finally stepping into it.

The Crash

On with it……..

There were three of us. We called ourselves TLC – an acronym for Three Ladies Cycling but committed to Tender Loving Care of each other throughout this physical challenge. Mimi, Tara, and I were riding the Great Divide Mountain Bike Route (GDMBR) from Canada to the US/Mexico line. We would be on our bicycles hour after hour, day after day, week after week, up to three months. That was the plan.

Steve had quit before we started. We were not his "tribe" and that was OK. Three independent older women and an "old school" former salesman perhaps would not have gelled.

Older women often become invisible, especially once we're no longer tied to a career, no matter how important it once was. We are irrelevant and I am finding that my friends are embracing it, embracing their true selves. Comfortable in our being, having let go of anything to prove, the children are adults, the husbands are content, and we can invisibly live our dreams.

Being invisible is freeing. Quitting my job was freeing. I was trapped, until I wasn't. Trapped in my mind, by the ingrained societal expectations of my upbringing. My women friends are now relevant unto themselves. And so, we rode…

Fuck, Fuck, Fuck! I turned around and rode back. "What can I do?"

Tara said, "Get the bike off her."

I stood stunned. I was 50 yards ahead when I heard it. I can still hear it—Mimi going down. It was like a thud combined with a splat, like a bag of wet cement hitting the pavement, followed by nothing, no skidding, no metal crunching, no screams of pain or cries of dismay, just the thud, then silence. I instinctively knew it was disastrously bad. My gut clenched. Had there been any food in my stomach, it would have come up from the revulsion of the sound of her body hitting the solid gravel road. I braked, stopped and looked back. Tara was climbing off her bike and kneeling beside Mimi. I quickly rode back.

This is catastrophic, I thought. *Why isn't she moving? She must be unconscious, or is she dead?*

We had been cruising fast for fully loaded bikepacking bikes, maybe twelve miles per hour, down a long descent, on gravel. We were dodging potholes in the mid-afternoon heat, about forty miles from Fernie, British Columbia. Our planned destination had been Weary Creek, but we were already getting stronger. So, when we passed Weary Creek mid-afternoon, we decided to push on toward Elkford.

"Let's get the bike off her," Tara repeated, as it would take two of us to lift the fully loaded, eighty-pound bike from atop Mimi.

Focus Jenny, I said to myself. We began lifting the heavy bike off Mimi's limp body, and without any consideration for the bike, left it on the road. We knelt, fearful of discovering the injuries on Mimi's inert body.

"Mimi, Mimi", "Talk to me Mimi", shouted Tara as she began the verbal arousal technique we learned in our first-aid classes for an unresponsive person. As Mimi did not respond to Tara's verbal requests, she began to apply a sternum rub, rubbing her knuckles on Mimi's sternum, attempting to arouse her by causing a painful stimulus.

"I take direction well, tell me what I can do to help," I said.

"Set off the Garmin® rescue device," Tara said.

"Where is it?" I said as I frantically looked over at Tara's bike.

"It's clipped on my water bottle bag, near the handlebars on my bike," she said.

My heart was racing and my breath was coming faster as the adrenalin hit my bloodstream. We were both visibly shaking, as the adrenaline coursed through both of us. I found the Garmin inReach® rescue device on Tara's bike and pushed the SOS button. I didn't know how to respond to the resulting query on the tiny screen. The responding message on inReach® said "cancel?" which was not intuitive to me as I was not thoroughly familiar with the device. Do I say "yes" or "no"? Cancel what? Would that cancel my request for help? Or bring me to another screen with another option for communicating? There was so much confusion at that moment, and yet everything seemed to unfold in slow motion.

Tara had inadvertently set off the device the previous day, and it had presumably sent a text to her husband, Larry. Tara had then quickly sent him a text directly, to say that we did not have an emergency. We never heard anything from that situation and had not thought any more about it. The InReach® device theoretically sent a notice to the primary emergency contact we had programmed into it, but it was never received, as we had input Larry's phone number into the device incorrectly. Hence, no notice to or from Larry had registered the previous day. The second contact was Raya, Tara's daughter, and she had received today's emergency alarm message. The rescue service had also called Raya and asked if she was in contact with her mom, and whether she knew if there was an actual emergency. Raya responded, "If she set off her emergency beacon, there is definitely an emergency." Thank you, Raya!

After I set it off, Tara grabbed her phone and opened the Earthmate® app that works in conjunction with the satellite unit. Through the app, we received a response from the service and confirmed that indeed, we needed help and rescue. There was still no response from Mimi. Her gasping, labored breaths continued while she was unconscious. *This is not good,* I thought to myself. *I think these are called agonal breaths which are the last gasping breaths taken by a person dying.* I thought *Mimi might be dying* but did not say anything as I was certain Tara was thinking the same thoughts.

At 61 years old, Mimi was our experienced trauma nurse. We had anticipated using *her* skills in the case of an emergency, but now, Mimi lay unconscious and unresponsive. What were the three of us doing out here, at our ages, miles from a town or people and amid Grizzly bear terrain in the Canadian Rockies? So much for trying to achieve one of our adventurous dreams and believing the fifties were the new thirties. Day three of riding and we were done. Now it was up to Tara and me to handle this awful nightmare of a situation. Steve, who was to be the lone man on this bicycle trek, backed out just before the trip began and there were no people, no cars, no anything in sight on the desolate, remote mountain road. We were alone, the three of us, none of us were Canadian citizens, and Mimi was still unresponsive.

As part of our preparation and training to bike the Divide (GDMBR), Tara and I had both recently taken a first responder first-aid course. As we had learned in class, when Mimi did not respond to any verbal stimulus, Tara continued trying to rouse Mimi by rubbing her sternum, increasing the pressure of the rub each time.

"Mimi! Mimi! Talk to me," Tara shouted, but Mimi was still unconscious. Periodically, her chest would balloon with deep, ragged breaths, then she would fall silent again.

As she rubbed her sternum harder and harder, Tara continued to say very loudly, "Mimi, Mimi, we need you to wake up Mimi!" At last, Mimi began to respond. A thin slit appeared between her closed eyelids, and we could finally see her eyes. Within a few minutes, which seemed like forever, the rhythm of Mimi's breathing normalized, the gasping breaths subsiding. Her eyes fully opened.

"What happened?" Mimi rasped.

"You crashed your bike," we replied. The words didn't register.

"What happened?" she asked again, still in a whisper.

Mimi was trying to make sense of her surroundings. I am not sure she even saw us.

Again, she asked, "What happened?"

We repeated the details of the accident several times. Each time, Mimi started over with "What happened?"

Tara and I glanced at each other, communicating our collective fear in the looks that passed between us. Clearly, Mimi's brain was still offline. Each time Mimi asked what happened, we indulged the question and repeated our responses. We spoke slowly, careful not to move her until we could assess her bodily injuries. Gradually, her singular question morphed into asking for more specifics. Finally, a good sign.

All this time, we were in the middle of the road, with no traffic and the sun beginning to move behind the mountains, the air cooling down. We prayed for traffic, prayed for someone who could help us to come along the desolate mountain road. We continually looked up the road, alternating searching the horizon for help with reassessing Mimi's condition.

Tara scanned Mimi's body while I checked the pupillary response of her eyes. Her pupils were equal in size and reacted similarly when opening and closing her eyelids. No brain swelling, yet. Despite an apparent puncture wound, there was no external bleeding. Tara and I were both worried about internal bleeding. *It's so much easier to treat leaks coming out from the body than it is to treat leaks pouring into the body.* Mimi tried to sit up, but we convinced her to lie flat and tell us what hurt. Her shoulder, her thumb, her side. With the pain in her shoulder, especially when she took a breath, and her extensive medical knowledge, Mimi jumped to the concern that she may have a pneumothorax—when air leaks into the space between the lungs and chest wall. She began to instruct us on how to use a safety pin to puncture her chest wall to relieve the building air pressure. Again, Tara and I looked at each other and communicated without speaking. *What?! A safety pin? Puncture your chest? We do not think so.*

Mimi's head was being held up by her helmet, creating a harsh angle between her neck and the ground. There was no question her helmet saved her life. We removed her helmet and used her fanny pack and a gear strap to fashion a neck collar, keeping her head aligned with her spine. Then we rolled her onto a sleeping pad to get her off the ground and make her more comfortable. Tara continued to relay information regarding Mimi's condition to inReach® search and rescue operators via the app.

I barely noticed my racing pulse and heightened senses. In the distance, I could hear the crunch of rubber on gravel, car tires slowly approaching from the same direction we had come. It was the truck we had seen at Weary Creek earlier that day.

I leaped to my feet and hailed the vehicle to a stop, although he could not proceed down the road with Mimi and our bikes covering the full width of the road, from ditch to ditch. A young man, who introduced himself as Brett, was driving.

"Can you help us?" I asked, talking fast and a bit breathlessly.

"What's happened?" Brett asked. He exited his truck, which he had parked directly in the middle of the road. Brett was the epitome of calm.

"My friend has been in a bike accident. She's badly hurt, and we need help getting her to the hospital." Brett quickly offered to help in any way he was able. "We were headed to Elkford, riding the Great Divide. Mimi tried to skirt one of those broad potholes. Her handlebars turned a bit too sharp, her front tire went sideways, and she flipped over the bike, with the bike coming down on top of her. She crashed onto her shoulder, head, and hand," I explained. "She has been unconscious and we have called Search and Rescue," I said in summary.

Mimi had returned to full consciousness and continued to self-assess her physical condition. With her consent, we decided to load the truck with our gear and if rescue had not yet arrived, we would put Mimi in the backseat of the truck and begin to go in the direction from which help was coming. Our goal was to reduce the time to get Mimi to more definitive care.

I removed the panniers and gear from our bikes while Brett reorganized his equipment, making room in the back of his small pickup truck for three large bicycles and the many bikepacking bags we were outfitted with. He had been on a solo fishing and camping trip and was returning home. Tara maintained contact with the rescuers through the app on her phone and continued to care for Mimi. Once the bikes and all our gear were somehow packed into the back of the truck, Tara, Brett and I decided to lay out a firmer sleeping pad and use it to lift Mimi into the back seat. It took a few minutes, but Mimi seemed stable, and we began driving down the road toward the ambulance. In a few miles, we intercepted the ambulance. Their protocols for moving someone with a possible head or spinal injury were far more rigid than the method we used to get Mimi into the truck. It took over an hour to maneuver her out of the truck, onto the stretcher, and into the ambulance. The fire service personnel said the prior year, during the GDMBR race, they had had to rescue several racers up here, mostly due to deep snow and hypothermia. With the heat today, at least we did not have to worry about hypothermia. That would come later for the three of us as we attempted to ride over Mount Lemmon in the Santa Catalina range in Arizona. Tara went in the ambulance with Mimi while I rode with Brett, who said he would take me into town to find a hotel. Fernie was the closest hospital, the closest town, the closest hotel, and that is where we went. Brett worked in a nearby mine and knew the area well.

The roads to Fernie were all dirt and gravel, and full of potholes. Traveling was slow and bumpy. Most of the local vehicles, Brett's included, have two-way CB-type radios and at regularly marked mileage intervals, the driver would talk into the handset, indicating their location and direction of travel. "Mile sixty-seven, headed south on Rt 467," he spoke into the ether. I assumed this setup allowed quick assistance to anyone in need of help or stranded on those remote roads.

"You and Tara have done a great job for your friend," Brett said. "Not just anyone would have known what to do in your situation."

"Thanks, but it still doesn't feel very good. We were lucky to have prior knowledge to draw upon. For several years, I volunteered for a search and rescue team in the White Mountains of New Hampshire, but it's been more than a half-dozen years since I have used those skills. Even back then, as a volunteer with a Wilderness EMT license, my main role was to take my turn carrying the patient in the litter. To be competent providing medical care takes practice and I never used the medical skills enough to feel practiced." "Tara is more experienced. She is a labor and delivery nurse" I said.

As a participant in both searches and rescues in the White Mountains of New Hampshire, I was familiar with the huge effort a rescue from the backcountry requires. I have always hoped to never be in a situation requiring the need to be carried out from the mountains. However, if you spend a good portion of your life outdoors and in remote locations, statistically your time may come. I fear that as my age continues to incrementally creep upwards, my chances of a future potential rescue are also increasing, so I try to be as prepared as possible. Having worked with a SAR team, I also know how long it takes for help to arrive. It can take many hours. Being prepared to care for yourself until help arrives is as important to your survival as the ability of rescuers to bring you back to civilization.

Poor Mimi—the pain and disappointment of training for years only to be going to the hospital and not the finish line—because her handlebars were particularly narrow and her bike, Pearl the Surly Girl, was squirrelly on gravel. As we drove, I worried about Mimi's condition and wondered, *what will Tara and I do now? Will we also go home and end this formidable effort to ride in two countries and across five states?* Again, I wondered, *what were we thinking?*

Finding a hotel was a challenge. Many of them were full, but Brett was patient, and I was forever grateful. He was a Godsend. On our third try, we finally found a hotel that had a room and the proprietor said we could bring our bicycles inside, but the room was on the second floor, up a set of steep and rickety stairs. Brett helped me carry each of the bikes and then many additional trips up and down the stairs with all the gear and bags. By the time Brett left, it had been dark for a while, but in town, I finally had cell phone service and called Tara for an update. Mimi was in the Emergency room, and the first question they asked her was "Do you have *Canadian* health insurance?" Oh shit.

The next day Tara and I each bought a Canadian health insurance policy. Calculating the cost per mile, since we only had two more days in Canada before we crossed the border back into the

United States, this was not a brilliant financial move. My trip budget took a hit.

We decided I should go to the hospital, so I carried my bike back down the rickety stairs. I added my light to be both visible and to see where I was going in the dark, and put a pannier back on so I could carry anything needed. Tara had asked for food. She eats a gluten-free diet, and we talked of finding some California rolls. I rode to a neighboring restaurant for take-out sushi and then I rode on to the hospital. It was dark and I was spooked, apprehensive about the passing cars and the potential for adding another accident to our crushing situation.

In the hospital, Mimi was assessed for alertness and lucidity by answering a series of questions. The doctor, a woman, said Mimi's head was fine and a brain scan was not needed. *Really?* The x-ray showed a broken collarbone, and her thumb was broken. Her helmet was damaged. It was not until she returned home to the States that her visibly broken ribs were noted on the x-ray. Mimi was still dizzy late in the evening, and they decided to keep her overnight, so Tara and I walked back to the hotel, pushing my bike, Blixen.

The gravel road. The "fucking" gravel road? No, that was not how I felt. I couldn't curse it. That was the adventure. To be on our bikes, riding on the gravel roads, for weeks at a time. Hour after Hour. Day after day. Week after week. This was supposed to be our happy place. Would it continue to bring happiness, fun and adventure or were we already finished, on day three of our lifetime dream?

The Worst Day of My Life

The worst day of my life wasn't on the Great Divide.

It happened years earlier, in the manufacturing plant I managed.

The plant had been purchased out of bankruptcy, and the employees were anxious, uncertain of their future, uncertain of me. I had been hired to rebuild the management team, to bring stability, to create a culture of safety and pride. The company was family-owned, with both paternalistic and maternalistic management styles, run by three aging brothers and a woman president. They believed in values, profit sharing, safety metrics, quality, and doing things the right way. I loved being plant manager for this Quebec based organization and my French language skills were improving.

John, the quality manager, is a great human being. Perpetually cheerful, always accommodating, a lifelong athlete who refereed hockey and basketball on the side. He was fast on his feet despite his build, and he and I had become friends. His wife and I kayaked together—mostly floating on quiet ponds, balancing wine glasses and cheese on the decks of our boats, laughing at how little paddling we did.

The morning of the accident, the management team had arrived early for a meeting. During a break, John went out onto the floor to check on production and greet the incoming shift. Somehow the forklift driver didn't see him.

The machine ran over his foot and leg. A degloving injury, the skin peeled away from the limb. Later, amputation.

I remember the helplessness. The shock. The way the world narrowed to a single point of horror. I remember being grateful for the employees who had been trained to respond to such a crisis. I remember thinking, *this cannot be happening.*

I remember the sound of my own heartbeat in my ears. Requesting a helicopter that was determined to be unnecessary.

The worst day of my life, still.

My parents had driven six hours to visit my husband, John, and me that weekend. We were supposed to go to the Adirondacks with friends. Instead, I spent the day at the hospital, then drove home in a fog of dread and exhaustion.

I called my parents from the car to tell them I would be late. In New York State, even then, it was illegal to hold a phone while driving. When the police officer pulled me over, I dissolved, sobbing, incoherent, apologizing. I don't cry, but that day I was a blubbering mess. I told him I was coming from the hospital. He let me go.

That day stayed with me. The helplessness. The responsibility. The knowledge that leadership sometimes means standing in the middle of a nightmare and doing the next right thing, even when you're shaking.

It was the day I learned that the body remembers trauma long after the crisis ends.

And on the gravel road in British Columbia, when Mimi went down, it wasn't a familiar fear that came back. It was that singular, once-in-a-career fear, the deep dread, that I might not be able to fix what mattered most.

Why Leave a Career and Ride a Bicycle for 2,700 Miles?

I quit the demoralizing job. I did. And then immediately thought, *OMG… what have I done?*

During the pandemic, anyone not working was labeled "lazy," "unmotivated," or "living off the system." I worried, briefly, that quitting might lump me into these categories. But honestly, I've never cared much about what people think of me, and I certainly didn't judge anyone who chose safety over exposure. So those weren't real reasons to stay. They were just the last flimsy excuses my brain tossed out before I finally admitted the truth: I wanted a different life. I had always wanted a different life.

It was late winter, early spring, (prime existential crisis season), when I decided, at fifty-six, that it was time to stop letting fear run the show. I wasn't getting any younger, faster, or more flexible. Recovery from even minor adventures was starting to take longer than the adventures themselves. If I wanted to chase the dreams I'd been collecting for decades, the time was now.

Being an engineer by training and temperament, I did what any self-respecting analytical overachiever would do: I made a list. A glorious, sprawling, deeply satisfying list. I even added things I'd already done, purely for the dopamine hit of checking them off. (If you know, you know.)

This list wasn't just chores or errands. It was the Big Stuff, the dreams I hadn't lived yet, the adventures I'd envied in books and magazines, the things friends and relatives were doing that made me think, *Take me with you!*

A few highlights:

Run an ultramarathon. (Because apparently 26.2 miles wasn't enough punishment.)

Backpack through Europe with a Eurail pass, drinking coffee slowly and walking everywhere quickly.

Hike the GR5 across the French Alps, from the Swiss border to Nice.

Ride the Great Divide Mountain Bike Route, from Banff, Alberta, Canada to the Mexico border, 2,700 miles of dirt, grit, and questionable decision-making.

Complete a half-Ironman. Swim 1.2 miles (I sink), bike 56 miles, run 13.1 miles. Why? Unclear. Blame Leigh for this one.

Finish all 48 of New Hampshire's 4,000-footers, despite having moved four hours away.

Write a book. Ha. Ha. Me? I am wordy, but in a purely social or strictly scientific, task-oriented way.

Simplify my life. (Still working on that one.)

Yes, I'm an overachiever. Yes, I'm a little crazy. And yes, I have a husband of 30 plus years who, so far, somehow tolerates all of this.

Financially, were we "secure"? Depends on who you asked. When coworkers accused John of being wealthy, he'd say, "I ate peanut butter and jelly for ten years so I could buy an excavator." And to be fair, that's not far off. He never bought lunch out, never went drinking with the guys, and his only indulgences were baseball caps and heavy equipment. Wealth is relative, and while we might not be rich in dollars by some standards, we're rich in family, whoopie pies, consistency, and the ability to laugh at ourselves. Still, the questions loomed: Could we live off savings and pie crusts until 67? Would Social Security even exist by then?

Meanwhile, my job, Director of Sales and Marketing in a toxic environment, was draining the life out of me. The final nudge came from an unexpected source: a quiet running friend who, during one of our 5:30 a.m. sanity-preserving miles, said, "You need to quit that soul-sucking job." It hit me like a brick. Why *was* I giving my best years to something that gave nothing back? And I had a LOT of dreams.

Mortality has a way of sharpening things, too. Friends in the medical field reminded me how fragile life is. My niece—26 years old, newly married, vibrant—was diagnosed with a brain tumor three weeks after her wedding. If I was going to live my dreams, WHEN exactly was I planning to start?

I'd always admired people who took long leaves from work to adventure. I even approved a two-month leave for an employee to bike across the U.S. But me? I never dared ask. Responsibility is practically my birthright, a classic middle-child trait, or perhaps ingrained Catholic guilt. I was completely committed to my employers, but why?!

Case in point: I once trained all summer for the Wildman Race - run, then bike, then run up Wildcat Mountain—only to be told at the last-minute that I *had* to attend a work meeting that Saturday. The company owner was flying in from Oregon. I showed up for the meeting, missed the race, and got to hear in person that the mill was shutting down and we were all losing our jobs. I sacrificed a summer of training and my race for that message. Even still, I stayed loyal to employers for decades afterward. If there were awards for committed responsibility, I'd have a shelf full of them.

The hardest part of quitting wasn't the money. It was the guilt. The fear of being "irresponsible." The 2 a.m. heart-racing panic about giving up a paycheck but more so, abandoning the people, the customers, the projects. But eventually, clarity won.

I did it. In my mid-fifties, in a post-pandemic world, I became one of those "unemployed, lazy individuals" who simply refused to give any more life to corporate nonsense. Gulp. John, ever grounded, supported me completely, even if he didn't always join my adventures. With his blessing, I stepped into the unknown.

Was I retired? Not really. Too young, not wealthy, and still responsible for our health insurance. But I had a plan: move my body, chase my dreams, and check off that list of dreams, one adventure at a time.

I've always been in motion. My college roommate once said I was a cross between a hamster on an all-night wheel and Speedy Gonzales. A friend's dad called me a hummingbird, constantly zipping around, unaware of how much fuel I required. I take both as compliments and accept their truthfulness.

And thanks to my friend Tara, one dream rose to the top: ride the Great Divide Mountain Bike Route from Banff to the Mexican border. If "early retirement" had a purpose, then this was it. Live the big dreams before my body staged a rebellion.

So off I went, into one of the most audacious adventures of my life.

Who to Blame

Like most questionable life decisions, this one started with a slideshow.

In 2020, Big-Ring-Bob, a friend of ours completed the Great Divide race and later inflicted (sorry, *shared*) his adventure with a group of friends via PowerPoint. There were photos of mud, mountains, exhaustion, and joy. Tara watched this presentation and, instead of thinking, "that looks horrific," immediately warmed to the idea of a three-month bicycling suffer-fest.

Tara has a long résumé of big adventures; India, high-mountain passes, nights without oxygen or sleep. She has battled hypothermia, mechanical failures, and saddle sores, but conveniently forgets all that when a new idea involves bikes and suffering. What she remembers is the movement.

She began actively recruiting co-adventurers, speaking with the enthusiasm of someone who had apparently forgotten her own history with pain and suffering.

It is important to note here, clearly, definitively, and for the historical record, that it was TARA who first floated this trial balloon. Because in the aftermath of any great escapade, it is critical to know who to blame.

Surprisingly, several friends, colleagues, and acquaintances expressed interest in riding the length of the Continental Divide by bicycle. Every one of them was crazy. In my usual exuberant fashion, I was the first to commit and never wavered, which should have been a red flag to everyone involved.

The questions came quickly: Who will go with us? (Answer: anyone foolish enough to say yes.) When will we go, next summer or the one after? And are we serious about this? (Yes. Unquestionably so.)

Eventually, the group filtered down to four people who possessed the necessary combination of desire, ability, finances, time, and poor judgment. In addition to Tara, there was Steve from Boston, a friend of hers from the Boston Cycling Club; Mimi, also from the club and conveniently employed at the same hospital as Tara; and me, recently relocated from New Hampshire to Maine. I didn't know either Steve or Mimi at the time, but I trusted Tara implicitly, which again brings us back to the blame issue.

I've always been enamored with people who know absolutely nothing about a sport and make a rash decision to attempt something legendary. You know the type: kayaking in the Arctic with no experience or buying a backpack and hiking the Appalachian Trail having never hiked before. These people are either insane or destined for greatness, sometimes both. They shouldn't survive, yet many of the stories I've read chronicle their successes.

Our approach, unfortunately or fortunately, was the exact opposite. With my background as an engineer and project manager, we leaned hard into planning. There were spreadsheets. So many spreadsheets. Detailed lists, gear testing, obsessive research, and long conversations with Bob, who had already completed the ride twice and kindly refreshed our bike-maintenance skills while literally jumping up and down with excitement for us. He was a wealth of information with a mind that could recall specifics of the trail in excruciating detail. He did not, however, dwell on the cold, frightening, or miserable sections we would encounter.

From the time I left my job until the start of the ride, we had about eighteen months to prepare. That time was filled with planning logistics, buying equipment (then rebuying better equipment), training our bodies for prolonged abuse, planning for our homes and families in our absence, and, of course, acquiring the bikes that would carry us into both glory and despair. Steve and I were already retired, which simplified things. Tara and Mimi still had to negotiate leaving their jobs, which required planning, courage, and probably some carefully worded emails.

The Divide, our chosen adventure, roughly follows the Continental Divide of North America. It stretches about 2,700 miles from Banff, Canada, to Antelope Wells, New Mexico, winding through the Rocky Mountains on dirt roads, forest tracks, remote trails, and the occasional place where you question all your life choices. It passes through rugged wilderness, high-mountain passes, and small rural towns. It is self-supported, physically demanding, mentally exhausting, and staggeringly beautiful.

The route can start in Jasper or Banff. The ride between the two is stunning, but also traffic-heavy and dangerous, so many riders opt to start in Banff.

There is an annual race in June with a couple dozen riders, many of whom are among the fastest off-road cyclists on the planet. For perspective: ultra cycling legend Mike Hall completed it in 13 days, 22 hours, and 51 minutes in 2016. In 2023, Lachlan Morton somehow did it in 12 days, 12 hours, and 21 minutes, which seems less like cycling and more like teleportation.

Consistent with the guidebook, we had planned for about ten weeks, give or take a few days. I would have been happy to plan a slower, more time-consuming trip, while Tara talked about possibly riding higher mileage, and thought we could finish in fewer days. (This will surprise no one who knows her.)

The route itself breaks down roughly like this: 257 miles in Alberta and British Columbia; 710 in Montana; 72 in Idaho; 489 in

Wyoming; 545 in Colorado; and, 701 in New Mexico. Total: 2,774 miles, depending on whose math you trust. About 70% of it is on county, Forest Service, and BLM dirt and gravel roads. In short: mostly dirt, often remote, occasionally brutal, and entirely unforgettable.

Getting to Banff, A Journey in Itself

Tara, Mimi, and I had planned to meet in Banff, Alberta, on Sunday night, August fourteenth, (2022) before embarking on the Great Divide Mountain Bike Route. Our plan had been to ride from Banff, Alberta, to Antelope Wells, New Mexico, following the route mapped by the Adventure Cycling Association, crossing the spine of the Continental Divide roughly 30 times and climbing 200,000 feet. We hoped to start after two days in Banff, organizing and packing.

Tara had traveled a few days earlier with her husband Larry as they were celebrating an anniversary. Mimi and I had planned to travel together from Boston.

Traveling there, however, proved to be a comedy of airline challenges and our first lesson in flexibility. Two weeks before departure, our flight from Toronto to Calgary was canceled (yes, just canceled), forcing us to rebook. In the rebooking shuffle, Mimi and I ended up on separate Boston flights, which we adjusted so we could fly together—but that flight was delayed. We missed our connection in Minneapolis and spent the night there. I was tired and we did not venture out for the evening, much to my regret. The next day we flew west to Portland, Oregon, well beyond our intended destination. We then circled back to Calgary. The extra miles were frustrating, but the aerial views of Mount St. Helens, Mount Hood, and Mount Rainier were spectacular.

From Calgary, we hired an Uber to take us to Banff, hoping to save a bit of time instead of taking the bus. Cost versus convenience was always a comparison while traveling, as saving time generally costs money. Our timesaving $10 "shortcut" turned into an extra half-hour when the driver had to stop and charge his electric vehicle.

Karma, clearly, for our massive carbon footprint. Eventually, we rolled into Banff to a warm welcome from Tara and Larry, who had prepared a delicious dinner. After two days of flights, missed connections, and circling the continent like migratory birds, we finally felt like adventurers, having finally arrived at our "starting" point.

That evening, we walked around town, savored the fresh mountain air, observed the resident elk population, and tried to quell our anxiety. Tomorrow we would pick up our bikes in Canmore, pack them, test ride them, and try to convince our legs and minds that climbing thousands of feet while carrying 75 pounds of gear was a good idea. If time allowed, we hoped to visit Lake Louise, a scenic reward before we traded sidewalks for singletrack. The weather was perfect, our spirits high, and despite the travel chaos, the adventure had officially begun.

Three Types of Fun

On a trip after attempting the GDMBR, we experienced our first Type III adventure.

Snow blew sideways across the road, my shoes squished with every pedal stroke, and I remember thinking, *This is not fun.* Not Type I, not Type II, nowhere close. There is an entire taxonomy for this kind of misery, and this was my first full-on Type III experience. I was cold, wet, and questioning every decision that had led me to that mountain. Why hadn't I spoken up more forcefully when we discussed our options for the day?

Because…ego. Because wanting to belong is powerful. Because no one wants to be the person who says "stop" and then wonders later if that choice had cost the group a great adventure. Because Tara and Lois were eager to continue, and disappointing them felt worse than the weather. Jon was more conservative, like me. Mimi was ambivalent or deferential, knowing she was the slowest, but she was always game for a hard day. Because we didn't have the right configuration of tents to split into two groups, even though we talked about it. Because I did not want to be responsible for shutting down the day.

Among adventurers, there is a universally accepted—though highly subjective—classification system known as the "Three Types of Fun." It describes the full spectrum of experiences, from delightful to disastrous. It exists for one purpose: to help us justify questionable decisions after the fact.

Type I Fun

Type I fun is, quite simply, fun fun fun. It is fun while planning, fun while doing, and fun while reminiscing. The activity doesn't matter—travel, hiking, biking, running, kayaking—as long as it includes good food, laughter, manageable discomfort, and memories that reliably make you smile.

Type I trips are a delight from start to finish. You look forward to them, enjoy them in real time, and glow when you talk about them afterward.

Examples of Type I fun:

- Kayaking with friends on a large lake in Maine. Challenging and wet, but joyful, with excellent companions and zero existential dread.
- Short running races: temporary suffer-fests followed by euphoric coffee-and-pastry celebrations where everyone agrees they "love running" again.
- Wandering through Europe with a niece, schedule optional. Museums, pastries, parks, the opera, boat rides, sunshine, and breakfasts by an open Airbnb window with a breeze off the water. The gold standard.

Type II Fun

Type II fun is trickier. It isn't necessarily fun while it is happening, but it becomes very fun later, once you are warm, fed, and safely home.

These trips are difficult. Someone may cry. The food might be terrible, insufficient, or both. You are cold, tired, hungry, and occasionally questioning your own character. You wonder if you have the mettle to finish. These moments are interspersed with laughter, fleeting joy, awe at the landscape, deep appreciation for your hardcore friends, and phone calls home to your very supportive husband, mainly to confirm that yes, he still loves you and will still be there when you return from yet another adventure.

In retrospect, the misery fades. What remains are wondrous memories:

- A spectacular sunrise over a mountain.
- A bicycle coated in frost while camping in the desert.
- Laughter over catastrophically bad food decisions.
- The time your dish soap was the same color as your olive oil and you sautéed onions in it.

Type II trips produce some of the best stories. The suffering is brief, but the dopamine hit at the end, the sense of accomplishment, is glorious.

Hiking the GR5 through the French Alps had been largely a Type II adventure. For my niece Leigh, it was definitely Type II. The packs were heavy. One day I needed help removing my wet clothes because I was flirting with hypothermia. There was recovery time. There was a strategic retreat to Cinque Terre. There was crying. But, there were also moments of spectacular scenery, elation, and pride. That is Type II fun.

Type III Fun

Type III fun is…not fun. Not during, not afterward, not even in hindsight.

The planning is exciting. The execution is painful. The idea was probably bad, the plan is flawed, and yet you do it anyway. Type III adventures are the ones where, in the moment, you genuinely fear serious consequences—hypothermia, frostbite, or death. You survive, but the limited fond memories are tinged with guilt: for making a poor decision, for going along with the crowd, for ignoring your gut. No laughter. No warm glow. Just a quiet agreement to never speak of it again.

For some of us, our ride over Mount Lemmon in Arizona during a snowstorm had been unequivocally Type III fun.

We had been on a bike trip in southern Arizona, the first part along a route called *The Islands in the Sky*, near the Mexico–Arizona border. We had started with seven riders; two had bailed after three days, citing extreme difficulty, brutal terrain, and a level of suffering they had not signed up for. Were we hardcore or were they wimpy? We decided we were "mostly normal," which was what people say when the evidence is inconclusive.

That left five of us. Tara, Mimi, Jon, Lois and I.

After finishing the route with a couple of days to spare, we made the fateful decision to ride up and over Mount Lemmon.

The first night had ended with a spectacular sunset and some deeply unsavory neighboring campers. Day two was warm and dry. The forecast was not. We debated our options at length, even flagging down a passing motorist—an act so unlikely it felt like divine intervention. They had a map, and with it we sketched a bailout plan.

By afternoon, that plan had expired. Once we rolled past the final turnoff to the last town, our choices narrowed to two: go up and over Mount Lemmon, or turn back, return to town, and almost certainly miss our flights home.

At the gas station, we stocked up and made the regrettable decision to continue. The variables were our speed—Mimi's especially—and a forecast that worsened with every thousand feet of elevation., and the climb, topping out at 9,000 feet.

That night we camped among an enthusiastic four-wheeling community. We started early the next morning. The riding was difficult, relentlessly uphill, and miserably cold. The snow started earlier than anticipated. And then, they left us.

Tara and I had ridden ahead initially, climbing as rain turned to snow. We regrouped a few times. Eventually, as the day wore on, Tara pushed ahead. I stayed with Mimi, concerned about her mental state, her physical strength, and the very real risk of hypothermia.

Jon and Lois also rode ahead, more experienced and stronger, moving faster to keep themselves warm.

I could have ridden faster to stay warm. Mimi could not. Her bike was heavy, the snow was wet, the wind blew sideways. Our shoes were soaked and squishy, and we burned through every hand and foot warmer we had. This part is still hard to reflect on.

If Tara hadn't reached the top hours ahead of us, we never would have found the Mt. Lemmon General Store and Gift Shop, a beacon of warmth, dry socks, cocoa, and survival. No one died that day. But I still wonder: if I had pushed ahead too, would Mimi have made it alone? Would she have found that store? Would I have found that store on my own? Would I have kept up with Tara? It wasn't our strength I doubted, or our ability to push through physically challenging situations, it was the way hypothermia creeps in, quiet and disorienting, before you realize what's being taken from you. Hypothermia is insidious that way.

This question, "Do you leave someone who is struggling?" is a fault line in the adventuring world. Some people continue on, assuming everyone is responsible for themselves. Search and Rescue trained that instinct out of me, or maybe it simply validated what was already there: stay, help, put your plans aside. But I am still to this day, learning to weigh the broader risks, to support a team decision even when my gut wants to anchor myself to the injured person, one not in our party, and refuse to budge.

As we climbed, soaked and numb, we planned to take refuge in the unmanned fire station at the summit. We imagined warmth. We imagined rest. When we finally approached the crest of the last hill, Tara appeared above us, an apparition in the gauzy curtain of snow. For a moment, we weren't sure if she was real or something we had hallucinated.

She urged us onward, downhill, into the wind, for just a few more minutes, to the store. After warming up, we changed clothes at the Mt. Lemmon Community Center, huddling under bathroom hand dryers like survivors of a shipwreck. Tara pushed us to keep moving. With twenty-eight miles still to ride, and daylight fading, she was right to push.

We stopped the last vehicle headed down in the storm and asked them to notify the Sheriff's department that we felt we were in trouble. We did not set off our Garmin InReach® rescue device; we were not yet that desperate. Or so we thought.

We made it down a road now officially closed due to the storm, riding through inches of slush. Twice we stopped in concrete pit toilets to do jumping jacks and eat gummy worms. The gummy worms saved us. We never did see a sheriff.

We never activated the rescue device. We made it back to Tucson alive, found a grocery store and Starbucks in which to recover, and Tara experienced a time warp. She asked the barista, "What time is it?"

"Six p.m.," he said.

She asked again, "What time is it now?"

"Six p.m.," he repeated.

Tara looked bewildered. She was convinced our ride had been hours shorter, that it was still early afternoon, when we had been out there battling the storm far longer.

For Mimi, Tara, and me: Type III fun. Not to be repeated. For Jon and Lois, a tough adventure, but not one considered life threatening.

After Mount Lemmon, we knew exactly what Type III felt like. The Divide would test us too, but in different ways. Could we do it? Would it be fun? What type of fun would it be?

As it turned out, our ride on the Divide was a blend of Type I and Type II fun, except for the accident, which was a singular Type III day. It was often uncomfortable: heat, cold, rain, and a steady diet of gas-station "food" consumed in heroic quantities. But the spectacular days far outweighed the discomfort.

And unlike Mount Lemmon, we wanted to talk about it afterward.

Chapter 2: Building the Courage to Begin

Reunited with Our Bikes

Day 0 - Tuesday, August 16
15 miles today
(Preliminary miles didn't count toward our total)
Starting in: Canmore - Ending in: Banff

We were reunited with our bikes yesterday at Rebound Cycles in Canmore, Alberta. We'd shipped them ahead using a bike shipping company called Bikeflights, sending them straight to the local shop for last-minute modifications and safety checks. Tara had traveled with her bike, arriving ahead of Mimi and me. Shipping was expensive, but we didn't want to risk delays. Honestly, missing my bike might have been a blessing, because a bikepacking trip without bikes is the only scenario where I might keep pace with Tara, a slower hiker than me.

Each of us had named our trusty steeds: Una (Tara's), Pearl the Surly Girl (Mimi's), and Blixen (mine). We would soon learn that Pearl truly was surly, as in bad-tempered, but before her true nature revealed itself, all three bikes were lovingly pampered by Emmanuel, a mechanic at Rebound Cycles. He converted our tires to tubeless in deference to the much-feared "goatheads," notorious for puncturing tires ceaselessly along this route and apparently existing for no other purpose.

Goatheads come from a plant called *Tribulus terrestris*, whose sharp, spiny seed pods resemble a goat's head with horns, adorable in theory and evil in practice. They puncture tires with enthusiasm and are also known as "puncture vine" or "devil's thorn," which we confirmed is an apt moniker.

Tubeless tires, as the name implies, have no inner tube. Instead, they're filled with a thin film of liquid sealant—ours was the brand called "Stan's." When a tire is punctured, the goo seeps into the hole and seals it almost instantly. We'd heard plenty of stories about riders battling goathead thorns and were relieved to have all our tires converted. We still carried spare tubes for emergencies, such as a torn tire or when the universe simply decided to test us. This was the final modification before mounting our steeds for the adventure. After reassembling the bikes, Emmanuel completed a full safety check.

We also purchased spare brake and shifter cables, bear spray (comforting but slightly alarming), new reading glasses for Mimi, and small containers to repackage food, because nothing says "long-distance cycling" like obsessing over snack logistics. After coffee, we rode the 15 miles back to Banff, where the GDMBR officially begins, and settled into the Airbnb for a couple of nights.

The bikes felt great. The mountains were spectacular—haze pooling in the valleys, softening the far peaks and giving the whole range an air of mystery. In reality it was smoke, and watching for forest fires would become a daily ritual.

Back at the Airbnb, we assembled and attached pannier racks, then organized and packed our panniers. Because airline delays had made us a day late, we felt pressure to complete in one day what we'd planned for two. It added stress and didn't leave time for the sightseeing we'd hoped for. Larry headed to the local bike shop and borrowed a pedal wrench from the owner, Tom. Later, as we walked to a great Mexican dinner, we ran into Tom again. He offered any help we might need until we reached the U.S.–Canada border. You must love small towns and the wonderful people in them, especially when they lend you tools and moral support.

We would soon learn that this friendliness and generosity were constants along the route.

After dinner, and a couple liters of beer for Mimi and Larry, margaritas for Tara and me, we stopped at the IGA for our final food supplies. We stayed up far too late packing and repacking, trying to make sense of our gear and our nerves. Larry would be heading back to Boston in the morning, and we would miss him dearly: chef, webmaster, handyman, bike mechanic, and, did I mention mental health counselor? We were so grateful for all Larry's contributions to our adventure.

At last, we were ready and it felt like graduating from college. Years of planning, training, lists, gear tests, and second-guessing all funneled into this single moment of readiness. We weren't dreaming about the ride anymore. We were finally standing at the edge of it, tired, a little behind schedule, but absolutely ready to go.

My earliest memories of bicycles include one with a banana seat and ape-hanger handlebars. We could fit three kids on one bike, no helmets, often barefoot. We just made sure to keep our toes out of the spokes. Later, I graduated to a shiny brown three-speed, and just before college I bought a brand-new twelve-speed for my first triathlon.

My first memory of a "long" bike adventure was as a teenager in the 1970s. My family spent summers "at camp," as we called it, on my cousin's property in a camper on Cobbossee Lake in Monmouth, Maine. My parents allowed me and a friend to ride ALL THE WAY from our home in Gardiner to camp. It took us all day, and I remember stopping at a dam to soak our hot feet in the water. It felt like a BIG adventure—and now I realize it was all of twelve miles. Even then, I dreamed big.

Later, as an adult, I biked across Maine, ending in the town of Cutler, to count snails for a friend of my parents' research project. Even then, I was pursuing the same two dreams I'd always had—long adventures and work that connected me to the environment.

BEARS

Everyone asks about bears. I am afraid of many things, but bears are not high on the list. I've had enough encounters over the years that the fear becomes familiar. That said, we were cautious. In New England we know black bears; grizzlies are another animal altogether, and we saw plenty of them. It was a dry season, and they were down in the valleys looking for food.

There's a saying about black bears, brown bears (grizzlies), and polar bears: *If it's black, fight back. If it's brown, lie down. If it's white, good night.* We would be riding through "fight back" and "lie down" country, hoping we'd know which was which in the moment.

We bought large cans of bear spray in Banff, about $40 each, and carried them religiously. We'd read stories of riders who kept them on their handlebars and wore a hole in the can, which did not end well. On a future trip across British Columbia, Tara would learn that lesson firsthand. That's a story for another time.

At night, we kept the spray on our person. One evening in a campground we heard a commotion and learned the next morning that the young group near us had accidentally set off their bear spray inside their tent. Alcohol may have been involved.

We saw our share of bears, both grizzlies and black bears, starting on the very first night. Then more on the second day. Soon we were conditioned to see them everywhere: in trees, in the brush, hulking around bends in the trail. In our minds, they were omnipresent. There were likely far more than the ones we spotted.

A few moments stand out, one with me yelling loudly. Another with Tara encouraging me to just "keep going". Other days we detoured around trail closures due to bear activity, and many times motorists stopped to warn us of bears in our vicinity.

We carried the spray until Pinedale, Wyoming. I was still feeling desperate to shed weight, my bike felt heavier with every mile, so I left mine at the Jackalope Motor Lodge, in the communal box of abandoned canisters, the first place it felt "safe" to part with it. Tara kept hers a few more days, ultra-cautious and stronger than me, unconcerned about the extra weight.

We saw more bear poop than bears, but one black bear did run up a tree directly in front of us. Thankfully, all the grizzly sightings were north of Pinedale, and according to the guidebook, there are no grizzlies south of Pinedale. I'm sure the bears have read the guidebook

Despite all the real and imagined bears, we never had a truly frightening close encounter.

Planning the Planning

As the four of us began preparing for this adventure, we quickly realized that quitting our jobs was only the first step. We still needed bikes, gear, maps, and a mileage plan(minor details, really).

We bought *Cycling the Great Divide* by Michael McCoy and the Adventure Cycling Association, which promptly reminded us just how big this undertaking was. The book broke the route into 70 days and included recommended campsites, water sources, gear lists, daily summaries, and turn-by-turn directions. I like details. I like plans. This book together with Bob's suggestions was like a hand-drawn map from an old explorer, every ridge, river, and hidden danger sketched in with care so you can walk into the unknown with confidence instead of guesswork.

Early on, Tara floated the idea of finishing in fewer than 70 days, with higher daily mileage totals. This frightened me. I was leaning toward fewer miles and a more leisurely trip, preferably one that didn't involve collapsing into my sleeping bag each night, like a fainting goat at the sound of a car horn.

Naturally, I made a list. A list to plan for the planning that needed to be planned. With some trips, the planning is half the adventure. So, we started with a list:

- Bikes: a surprisingly important detail
- Maintenance tools and the knowledge to use them
- Gear choices: lots of gear or less gear (this debate would never truly end)
- Spare parts plus the tools to install them
- Navigation tools along with phones, lights, maps
- Clothing & essentials: helmets, shoes, toiletries
- Shelter: tents, sleeping pads, sleeping bags
- Food & water plus the cookware to prepare it
- Storage systems: racks & packs for our "essential" items
- Safety gear: bear spray, InReach Mini®, first-aid kit, emergency shelter
- Weather layers: for heat and cold (sometimes on the same day)
- Logistics: where we'd sleep each night

- Budget: best discussed vaguely
- Bike transport: ship them or carry them on the plane

Recognizing that all this planning would be completely useless if we didn't know how to bikepack, we also scheduled several "practice" trips. These were equal parts training, experimentation, and discovery—what we needed, what we didn't, and what we would never bring again under any circumstances.

I didn't have the right bike, but it was during COVID, and bikes were apparently rarer than toilet paper. Tara and I eventually decided to ride gravel bikes instead of mountain bikes, each having both benefits and drawbacks. Mimi, through a connection with her brother, managed to find and purchase a mountain bike, instantly making her the most prepared among us.

Gravel bikes typically have no suspension and narrower tires. They're faster and more efficient on smooth surfaces, but less comfortable when things get rough, which, on the Great Divide, they absolutely would.

Bob, the infamous rogue at the root of this entire quest, also owned a seasonal bike shop. He had a new gravel bike on order, a Canadian-made Devinci in exactly my size, due to arrive in the spring. I ordered it, sight unseen, buoyed by optimism and a healthy disregard for supply-chain realities in a pandemic.

Until it arrived, I practiced on whatever bikes I already had in my little fleet, hoping that enthusiasm and meticulous planning would make up for any bicycle deficiencies. Let's just say it was a learning experience.

Training

The Pannier Incident

I should have known the Great Divide would be trouble the day my pannier launched itself off my bike and tried to commit suicide on a gravel road in northern New Hampshire. One minute I was pedaling along, proud of myself for surviving the first few miles of my first "training ride," and the next minute I heard a dragging sound behind me, never a good sign on a bicycle. I looked back to see my pannier bouncing along the road like a reluctant toddler being hauled to daycare.

Tara, of course, was already fifty yards ahead, riding the bike she'd bought specifically for the Divide, looking competent and unbothered. I was on my old titanium Merlin, rebuilt because the bike I'd ordered was delayed. Bob had outfitted the Merlin with drop bars, two sets of brakes, and enough optimism to mask the fact the bike and I were both older than we wanted to admit.

We were now fifteen months from our planned departure date. Plenty of time, I told myself. Then the pannier fell off, and I revised that to: *We're doomed.*

We had packed tents and all our camping gear for that first overnight, riding from Tara's New Hampshire yurt to a friend's house. After pitching our tent in Paula's tick-infested field, we lasted about ten minutes before dragging our sleeping bags inside her house. Who chooses damp grass and ticks when there's a warm kitchen and a cooked meal? Not us. Not if it meant declining available and proffered comforts.

The next morning, we rode back to the yurt, my pannier reattached but my confidence only loosely so. Trip #1 completed and already a lot learned.

Campground Roulette

By late May of 2021, we were ready for our second training ride: northern New Hampshire into northern Vermont. "Ready" being a generous term. I was still riding the Merlin, still wobbling on gravel, still wondering what I'd been doing with my time for the past fifteen years while my panniers sat unused in my gear room.

We hadn't made camping reservations, assuming campgrounds would be open. They were not.

Our first campground attempt was a horror movie set: a car full of debris at the entrance, cabins vomiting belongings onto the lawn, overgrown tent sites, and no caretaker in sight. We left quickly, inventing our campground rating system on the spot. This one scored high on the fright scale.

Our second attempt was far up a long hill. It was late, we were tired, and the proprietor informed us they weren't officially open. The bathrooms were nonfunctional. Tara, the nurse, offered a detailed waste-management plan. The campground owner vetoed it.

We rode back down the hill.

Our final option was knocking on my coworker Steve's door. His yard was immaculate, grass trimmed to regulation height, apple tree in full bloom, petals drifting like confetti. On our new rating scale, this stop was a twelve plus. Hot showers, a kitchen, food, and the softest "tent camping" we would experience.

The next day we rode through the Balsams Resort, descended into Stark, lunched by a windy lake, and camped at Thirteen Mile Woods. The following morning was foggy, cold, and damp. We layered on all the clothing we had, stopped at a small inn to warm up, and eventually made our way back to the yurt. Tara recommended we take the long way. I trailed behind.

Sunrise Trail Misfire

Our third training ride was closer to my home, on the Downeast Sunrise Trail in "Downeast" Maine. The trail was soft, dusty, and crowded with four-wheelers. After a few hours, we decided it wasn't challenging enough, too flat and too busy. Combined with a poor weather forecast, we bailed and backtracked to a campground.

It rained. Friends drove over to camp with us. We had wine but no bottle opener. Marsha's husband had packed everything—canopy, grill, hammer—but not the wine bottle opener so, we borrowed one from a neighbor. The campground rated a "6", the neighbors, a "10."

The next day, we abandoned the weather system entirely and drove back to Boothbay, where we planned a reroute from my house to my sister's lake cottage, then to a campground, and back home. It turned out that learning to "reroute" would be a valuable skill.

The next day, my dad rescued me roadside after a rack and pannier malfunction. I acquired a new one while Tara continued to ride. We made it to the lake together, and my 8 year old niece put chocolates on our pillows, like a fancy hotel, but in a tent. The next morning, Tara was motion-sick from the morning coffee combined with a boat ride around the lake. That night, after a lot of uphill, her lower back seized, and we used a food pouch as a heating pad. Dual-purpose dehydrated meals.

Larry to the Rescue

Training ride number four took place in August 2021 and included Steve. We had planned a four-day tour of Vermont's Northeast Kingdom, but early in the ride Steve suffered heat stroke. Tara's husband, Larry, came to the rescue, retrieving him and getting him safely back to his car. Larry would go on to become our most reliable supporter, stepping in more than once. It became a theme.

Tara and I continued the ride, camping at a friend's cabin on a pond and supporting a lemonade stand run by two small children. It was charming, in the way things are charming when you're not the one with heat stroke.

We successfully rode four consecutive days and now consider ourselves practically experts.

Brattleboro Breakpoint

Our final shakedown ride was in May of the following year, the spring of 2022: a 137-mile circumnavigation of Brattleboro, Vermont. I had a new bike! All four of us went, the full team, our group planning to ride the GDMBR. We decided to stay in hotels as it was early season, the weather unpredictable, and the spring bugs were out. We didn't carry tenting equipment or make reservations as we were not certain of our daily mileage. Who needs reservations in May in Vermont? Apparently in a post pandemic world, we did.

COVID closures and limited availability left us scrambling. At one point, a pastor offered us a church basement. Mimi crossed the road to investigate an inn while Tara and I were simultaneously on our phones trying to problem-solve.

By the end of this adventure, Steve decided we were not the right group for him. He is a wonderful, chivalrous person, but traveling with three independent women may have left him feeling perpetually behind. I understood this completely. I once traveled through New Zealand with my niece and her husband, thirty years younger than me. I always felt a step behind as they made plans, reservations, and arrangements for the next stop, while I was still trying to unlock my phone.

After the training rides, our group went from four to three.

And the real adventure was still ahead.

Chapter 3: The First Miles Change Everything

The Riding Begins

Day 1 - Wednesday, August 17
22 miles today • 22 miles total
To Spray Lake

Tara once read that we should "pack for our fears." If that were true, our fears were apparently forged from metal—heavy, awkward, and impossible to ignore. Hunger, cold, bears, exhaustion: we had a piece of gear for every imagined disaster. By the time we finished strapping everything to our bikes, our anxieties had taken physical form, bolted to our frames in eighty-pound bundles of nylon, hardware, and waterproof zippers.

The real trouble started with my bike, Blixen. After packing, I took him for a quick spin around the block, expecting a reassuring glide. Instead, he shook like he was trying to rattle himself apart. Road riders call it the "death wobble," and Blixen had a terminal case. With the rear rack overloaded, he was a quaking, vibrating disaster waiting to happen. A cold knot tightened in my chest. *Can I do this? Do I have the wrong bike? Do I need all this heavy STUFF?*

I retreated to the Airbnb, hiding my I'm-about-to-die face from the others, and launched into a frantic round of trail-side physics. I stripped the bike bare, moved the heavy gear to the front panniers, shifted the lighter kit to the back, and attached a "junk drawer" bag onto the handlebars. Miraculously, Blixen settled down. On the next loop around the block, he rolled like a bike that wanted to live. Lesson learned early: on a 2,700-mile trek, weight balance isn't optional, it's survival.

My companions were having their own gear crises. Tara, anxious about her new tubeless tires, brought a mini pressure gauge she named Pierre. Tara names everything. Pierre was consulted with the reverence of an oracle. Mimi, meanwhile, worried about the hills and the sheer tonnage of her bike. Even before Mimi added her "essentials," Pearl weighed more than a small motorcycle. After we shipped a box of "unnecessary" items home via Larry, our rigs still weighed between seventy-five and eighty pounds. We weren't cyclists; we were pilots of two-wheeled tanks, which was concerning.

We said goodbye to Larry at 10:30 a.m. and then proceeded to move at the speed of a tectonic plate. We stopped in town for extra straps and a dry bag, then photos of a pink umbrella bike, then a final stop for more photos at the Banff Springs Hotel. If momentum were a currency, we were bankrupt. I hoped the whole trip would be this silly and scenic, even if we never made it to the Mexico border. I didn't yet know that after "the crash," whimsy would give way to grit as I fought to keep up with Tara's powerhouse legs.

We finally reached the start of the trail, behind the Banff Springs hotel, around noon. The Goat Creek Trail wasn't a road; it was a rugged mountain bike trail with stream crossings, narrow bridges, and rocks that seemed personally offended by our presence. With eighty-pound bikes, every climb felt like negotiating with gravity itself. We wrestled our way through the miles, learning to handle our heavy bikes, until Spray Lake finally appeared, a long, cold reservoir guarded by the jagged shark-fin silhouette of Shark Mountain. Throughout the challenges of our first afternoon, our emotions matched the weather, warm and sunny.

The campground was basic: a few sites, pit toilets, and a green hand pump labeled "BOIL WATER," which is the universal sign for "We haven't tested this, so good luck." We dutifully boiled pot after pot, burning through fuel, until we saw the campground host's wife drink it straight from the pump. We decided if she wasn't dead, we wouldn't be either. It was cold, delicious, and only slightly terrifying.

Our bear paranoia peaked at dusk. We wore helmets and carried bear spray just to ride to the water pump. On the final trip, Tara spotted one-a massive, furry, black shadow lumbering up the gravel road. She didn't use the spray. Instead, she rode back to camp singing at the top of her lungs, announcing her presence to the wilderness. If I'd seen it, I probably would've just hummed nervously and hoped for the best, as I truly can't carry a tune in a bucket.

As the sun dipped behind the Shark Fin, we washed in the lake, ate our dehydrated meals and collapsed into our sleeping bags. We were tired, we were heavy, and we were officially out there. For all the wobbling, the fear, the absurdity, and the weight, literal and otherwise, we had truly begun this much planned for and anticipated adventure!

Tara

If you spend any time with Tara, you learn quickly that she lives in a different athletic universe than the rest of us. If not cycling all day, a "light day" for her might involve swimming a casual mile or two or ten, followed by lifting weights, or, in winter, skiing for four or five hours. She does all this with the same expression most people wear while folding laundry. Effortless. Unbothered. Almost meditative.

Strength radiates from her, but not the loud, look-at-me kind. Hers is the quiet, durable kind that shows up in multiday bikepacking races where she is sometimes the only woman. When she lived in India, she entered a race and found herself up against the female national champion mountain biker. Tara finished ahead of her, of course, and then immediately used her nursing skills to treat the national champ for heat exhaustion. That's Tara in a nutshell: she'll beat you, then save you, then probably apologize for beating you, and then beat herself up for apologizing and not accepting her strengths.

Her toughness is matched only by her gentleness. She is the most selfless person I've ever met, which makes her an ideal bikepacking partner. She carries more gear weight than I do without complaint, shares food and water freely, and, when necessary, helps push my bike up hills that my legs have politely declined to participate in. She does all this with the calm of someone rearranging throw pillows.

I often think of her as Pippi Longstocking—thick red braids, a mischievous spark, and a strength that seems to defy physics. In local bike circles, she's known reverently as "Diesel," because she can ride in a low gear at a steady pace for days. Not hours. Days. She is the human equivalent of a reliable engine: consistent, unstoppable, and somehow still silly and cheerful.

Her competence is almost unsettling. I've watched her, cold and hungry, methodically unlink a chain to detangle it or coax a stubborn pedal off a bike as if negotiating with a small, unreasonable child. She never panics. She never snaps. She simply solves the problem, the way nurses do when the rest of us are losing our minds.

As a labor and delivery nurse, Tara had one very specific dream for this trip: to stumble upon a mom-to-be in distress so she could deliver a baby somewhere out in the wilds of the Great Divide. That was her fantasy scenario. Mine was not that.

Two years after riding the GDMBR, in the Arizona desert, we waited for a Search and Rescue helicopter to lift us and our bikes across the surging Gila River. Tara hates flying, but she went first, dangling from the extraction cable like a very athletic marionette. She kept her eyes closed the whole time, the rescuer told me later. When it was my turn, I felt something unfamiliar, gratitude maybe, or humiliation. Hard to tell, but I almost cried. Tara, meanwhile, simply dusted herself off and carried on. No drama. No tears. That's another rule with her: we don't cry. And no one dies. So far, so good.

Before our Great Divide trip, she entered a 250-mile north-country race. She was the only female and finished in two and a half days. Her longest day was 106 miles. She mentioned this casually, the way someone might mention picking up milk. She once told a doctor, "I'll never be mistaken for an Olympic athlete," which is true only in the sense that Olympic athletes might not be able to keep up with her.

Being around Tara means constantly recalibrating your definition of "normal." It means witnessing a person who is both steel and softness, endurance and empathy. It means watching someone move through the world with a kind of grounded power that makes you believe that most problems—mechanical, physical, existential—can be solved with patience, a multitool, and maybe a snack.

This is Tara: the diesel engine with red braids, the nurse who rescues the competition, the partner who carries the extra weight without mentioning it, the woman who will ride for days and still offer you her last sip of water.

If you're lucky enough to bikepack with her, you learn two things very quickly.

She is extraordinary.

And you'd better start pedaling.

Dusty and Grizzly

Day 2 - Thursday, August 18
37 miles today • 59 miles total
To Mt. Sarrail Campground

Today we rode between thirty-six and thirty-nine miles, depending on which navigation unit you believe. We have now officially ridden fifty-nine miles in total, or possibly more if we use the more optimistic GPS device.

We left Spray Lakes a few minutes earlier than our departure from the Airbnb yesterday. The morning was pleasant and the weather, once again, was perfection—warm, blue skies, sunshine. We are still working on the morning routine and packing process, and we are not yet super-efficient. Today the ride was completely different from yesterday, both in terrain and in views.

Most of the day was spent on Spray Lakes Road, which provides access to the national parks. Although very remote, it was surprisingly busy with traffic. The road surface resembled a washboard sprinkled with pea stones for extra excitement. We had to watch closely for potholes and loose gravel while also trying to admire the scenery and simultaneously scan the roadsides for bears.

Multitasking was essential and exhausting.

It struck me that this constant vigilance left little room for drifting thoughts. There was no mental space for anything beyond the present moment, no replaying yesterday, no planning tomorrow. The soft gravel road and the fear of bears demanded full attention, and in return offered a strange kind of clarity. Not peaceful, exactly, but enough to quiet the deep-seated fear that I needed to reduce my gear weight if I was ever going to make it to the border of Mexico.

If you drifted from the clear, rideable space in the center of the road to the shoulder, you had to cross what felt like an eddy line of four-inch-deep pea stone. Controlling a heavily loaded bike through soft stones provided a continuous flow of adrenaline. We rode slowly and pulled our bandannas up over our faces every time a car passed, all of us disappearing into a thick cloud of dust.

We were constantly making choices: blink the dirt out of our eyes, watch the road to avoid crashing, or scan the road shoulders for bears. We could only do two of the three at any given moment.

Just before stopping for lunch at a sparkling cold creek near Mount Engadine Lodge, we saw a grizzly cross the road from right to left. I had previously given very clear instructions not to yell "bear!" when spotting a grizzly. However, when it passed between Mimi and Tara, up ahead, and me trailing behind, I yelled, "Bear! Bear! Bear! Bear!" at full volume. Who heeds their own advice?

My excuse was that I didn't think Mimi and Tara were aware of the bruin and I wanted to alert them in case it turned their way. It climbed the left bank beside the road and wandered off, apparently unimpressed by my enthusiasm.

Shortly after lunch, on the same road, a larger grizzly wearing a leather collar stepped onto the road from our left, directly across from us. Tara calmly said, "Keep riding, keep riding," and we did, passing without incident. This was one of many moments when Tara's calm demeanor proved invaluable.

These encounters carried a quiet reminder that we were visitors here, moving through someone else's home. The bears didn't alter their pace or posture for us; they simply existed, while we adapted. It felt humbling to be so clearly insignificant in the grand scheme of things, especially knowing our place on the food chain.

Eventually we reached a paved road in Peter Lougheed Provincial Park and then transitioned onto a bike path for a few blissful miles. We stopped at the Bolton Creek Trading Post for ice cream, which felt both earned and necessary. Ice cream is my savior, at home and on the bike. This may be my greatest flaw, an addiction to ice cream. We chatted with other tourists, some who were surprisingly eager to hear about our adventure.

Beyond the trading post, the next section of the bike path was closed due to bear activity. It was only day two, and already bears seemed to be a recurring theme, rather than an exception. We returned to the road and continued riding, until we reached our destination, one of the Mt. Sarrail campgrounds.

Covered head to toe in dust, we took turns bathing under the campground water pump. The water was cold, bracingly so, and effective. We set up our tents with a beautiful mountain view and made dinner. The weather remained warm and dry.

Before settling in, Tara used Pierre to check her tire pressure as well as the tires on both Pearl the Surly Girl and Blixen. Pierre approved.

Mimi

If you want to understand Mimi, start at the Boston Public Garden. Look for the Swan Boats, those iconic, slightly whimsical vessels that have been gliding around the pond since 1877. Each one weighs about 6,000 pounds and is powered by a single captain pedaling atop a paddle wheel. Said captain, legs spinning beneath her like a Victorian-era Peloton instructor, might very well be Mimi.

There is something perfect about that image: Mimi quietly moving a massive boat full of strangers with nothing but her own consistent rhythm. She makes it look effortless, even graceful. That's her way in the world, propelling heavy things with a light touch.

Mimi is a city creature, elegant in a way that feels unstudied. She has shoulder-length white hair, blue eyes sparkling with mischief, and a willowy frame that belies her strength. At sixty, she carries laugh lines like jewelry—earned, cherished, and worn proudly. She is beautiful in the way people are when they've lived fully and refused to dim.

She has always had a kind of *joie de vivre,* a phrase she once used against herself, after the crash, as if enthusiasm were a liability. "Maybe I had too much *joie de vivre,*" she said. I couldn't shake that line for days. Mimi, doubting her zest for life? Impossible. She is the person who brings lightness into a room simply by entering it. She is silly and playful, the kind of woman who will laugh at herself before anyone else can, and who sees the world with curiosity rather than caution.

Her life is full. She has two grown children, including a son who splits his time between Mexico City and Germany with his partner, giving Mimi and her husband of thirty-five years an excuse to travel widely. She is a fan of Georgia O'Keeffe, drawn to bold color and unapologetic form. She plays soccer in a city women's league, rides with a Boston cycling club, and moves through urban life with a sophistication that I, a nature-leaning soul, can only admire from the sidelines.

And yet she is grounded, literally and figuratively. She drives an electric car, which once failed to charge fast enough to get her to our Adirondack departure on time. She arrived flustered but laughing, shrugging off the delay with the same good humor she brings to everything. Mimi has scars from past crashes but she wears them like stories, not warnings.

Underneath her lightness is steel. Mimi has spent her entire career as a critical care nurse, tending to traumatic injuries with compassion and competence. She is the person you want beside you when things go wrong—calm, clear-headed, and unafraid to act. Tara joked that we needed Mimi in case of bear trouble, but the truth is, we needed her for everything: her medical expertise, her troubleshooting instincts, her ability to stay soft in hard moments.

And then, suddenly, she wasn't with us on the trek anymore.

When Mimi stepped out of the journey, something subtle shifted. The miles moved a little quicker, and the air felt a little quieter. She had a way of keeping us laughing, of easing the strain without ever trying. Without her, the trail lost a bit of its playfulness. Only then did I understand how much her presence steadied me.

I missed her. Not just as a teammate, but as a counterbalance to Tara's diesel-engine power and my own anxious practicality. Mimi was the middle note, the harmony, the laughter between the miles.

Who is Mimi?

She is a woman who pedals 6,000-pound boats and makes it look easy.

A woman who packs too many gadgets and laughs about it.

A woman who has lived enough life to know what matters and enough joy to keep choosing it.

A woman who defies age, expectation, and gravity.

A woman who worries about retirement but never about living fully.

A woman who brings lightness to heavy places.

Mimi is, simply, a joy to be around. And when she steps out of the picture, you feel the absence like a shift in weather.

Weary Creek

Day 3 - Friday, August 19
32 miles today • 94.4 total
Mt. Sarrail Campground to Fernie Hotel

By the third day, I was still waiting for the Divide to show its softer side, as if the trail might eventually decide to be reasonable and let us settle into a casualness that we find when riding at home. It didn't. Every climb felt like a negotiation, every descent a small act of faith. I wasn't truly afraid, just learning the particular personality of this route, the way it demanded attention and respect. Discomfort for fun.

It brought me back to one of those early trips with my niece Leigh, eight years prior. Not because I was out of my depth, but because she had a way of expanding the world for both of us. Barcelona was one of our first big adventures together—narrow streets, late-night traditions, the Nose Man, the sour grapes we choked down well before midnight. We were two runners exploring a city on foot, discovering that movement was our shared language long before either of us knew how much we'd rely on it as the center of our adventures. Even then, she carried a quiet boldness, and I carried the curiosity that has always pulled me toward the next trail, the next challenge, the next horizon.

Without children of my own, I've grown closest to a few of my nieces. Leigh, especially, feels like the daughter I never had, only without the diapers, the teenage battles, or the emotional landmines. Instead, I get the rare gift of a relationship built entirely on compatibility. We both love to run, travel, and eat, which is a pretty solid foundation for joy.

When she was in college, we went to Barcelona to run the New Year's Eve Nose Run. It was one of our first big adventures together, and not one I would have chosen on my own. Big cities intimidate me; they feel chaotic and unpredictable. As an outdoor enthusiast, my ideal vacation involves national parks, quiet trails, and the possibility, however remote, of a bear encounter. I fear bears less than city people. But Leigh, even then, nudged me past the boundaries I'd built for myself.

She had always been interested in the far-flung regions of the world. As a homeschooled five-year-old, she could spin a globe and locate any country you named. Point to a random spot and she'd rattle off the capital. To this day, she knows capitals of places I still haven't heard of. Traveling with her meant stepping into a wider world, one she navigated with curiosity and confidence, despite her shy nature.

Barcelona offered its own magic. L'Home dels Nassos—the man of the noses—appears only on December 31st, with as many noses as days left in the year. Children expect a monster of hundreds of noses, but on the last day of the year, any ordinary passerby qualifies. I loved the whimsy of it, the way a culture can turn a simple wordplay into a tradition.

After the evening ten-kilometer race, we showered and put on the red underwear we'd packed to honor another Spanish custom. Red is supposed to bring luck and love in the coming year. Back then, Leigh was single and my husband of well over 25 years was steady and reliable, and I wasn't looking for new love. But it still felt fun and a little mischievous, to play along.

We bought the customary grapes, and champagne too. Las Uvas de la Suerte requires eating twelve grapes at midnight, one for each stroke of the clock, each grape a wish for the coming year. Ours were sour and full of seeds, and we didn't drink the champagne. We were asleep before midnight. The perfect traveling companion. I love her.

Since that first trip, we've traveled to other places, often choosing destinations with a race attached. We ran to the Hollywood sign in California, where another niece, Abi, joined us. They took a wrong turn and added extra miles while I ran ahead, blissfully unaware. In 2016 we ran the Crazy Horse Half-Marathon in South Dakota. The altitude, over 5,000 feet, worked us both over. After finishing, Leigh threw up in a trash barrel. We still laugh about it. Type II fun at its finest.

Running has always been our shared language. In Barcelona, I ran circles around her, filming her with my phone while chatting away. Today, years later, the roles have shifted. She's faster than I am now, but gracious enough not to rub it in. Yet I would not be dismayed if she ran circles around me the way I once did with her. I would laugh and keep running in an attempt to keep up.

Last night we stayed at the Mt. Sarrail campsite between Upper and Lower Kananaskis Lake. Morning greeted us dry and dust-free. Our tents were blissfully free of dew, a small but meaningful reprieve in our task-based morning routine. A dry tent is less weight, and less weight is critical for my mental outlook.

Before leaving camp, Tara performed some TLC on all our bikes, cleaning and lubing chains and, of course, checking tire pressures, again, with Pierre. By day three, Tara and Pierre had developed a regular routine, often engaging multiple times a day. Pierre took his responsibilities very seriously.

By the third day, small improvements in efficiency mattered. The anxiety of getting started was still with us, but we were settling into a familiar morning routine. Dry tents felt like the gods were smiling on us. Fear diminishes with rituals—small, repeatable steps that make the unknown feel less wild. Confidence thrives on them too. Somewhere between the chain lube and the tire gauge, preparation started to feel less like panic and more like care.

Our first three to four miles were up, up, up, with sections that required pushing our bikes toward the top of Elk Pass. At one point, Tara tipped over into a soft, bushy ditch while trying to ride, moving too slowly to stay upright. Thankfully, she wasn't hurt.

As Tara rode, Mimi and I struggled behind with our heavy bikes, straining to push them up the steep gravel path. We simply weren't as strong as Tara and resorted to pushing when our legs could no longer keep the pedals turning. As runners, we discovered that sometimes we were better at pushing than riding, a humbling but useful realization.

There is a particular vulnerability in pushing a bike uphill. You are exposed, slow, and undeniable in your effort. Riding can look graceful; pushing looks honest. That morning, strength wasn't about speed or style, it was about not stopping.

At the top of the pass stood a beautifully carved log post welcoming us to the Elk Valley. Mimi immediately jumped up and down, ringing a cowbell. We all performed our first Continental Divide Pass dance, something we would repeat atop many passes throughout the trip. Mimi was celebrating for her sister, whose inheritance had helped fund part of this adventure. The pass dance was ridiculous and joyful. We were doing it, riding the Divide, and life could not be better.

The Elk River is world-renowned for fly fishing, and we saw several fishermen camping in the valley. We followed a power line for a stretch and then descended a long, steep logging road. The landscape showed large swaths of logging at various stages of cutting and regrowth, some ragged and raw, others burgeoning with new life. The views were constantly changing.

The land mirrored how we felt, parts worn down, parts recovering, all of it still working.

The road rolled along with a series of hills on hard-packed gravel. We passed the Tober Morey cabin and stopped for a break. The cabin is maintained by users and open to everyone, but it was far too early in the day for us to stop.

Next, we encountered a large herd of horses used for packing trips. They roam freely on public land and regarded us with mild curiosity and total indifference.

We eventually stopped at a beautiful, rushing creek appropriately named Weary Creek. We soaked our feet, had snacks, and Mimi, true to her adventurous and fearless personality, went for a full dip in the frigid water. Cold water has a way of quieting fear. It replaces anxiety with sensation, forcing you fully into the present moment.

A truck loaded with camping gear sat nearby, but there was no sign of its owner. Within hours, we would be forever grateful for that fisherman.

The day was hot, the weather remained beautiful, and despite the climbing and pushing, our spirits were high. We had originally planned to stop at Weary Creek for the night, but it was still only mid-afternoon, and with the truck parked at the campsite, we decided to go a bit further.

Strength, we were learning, wasn't the absence of anxiety. It was the growing ability to move forward anyway—sometimes riding, sometimes pushing, and occasionally dancing at the top.

And then disaster hit.

The Aftermath of Day 3

Friday - August 19
32 miles today • 94.4 total
To Fernie Hotel

It was late on day three when everything changed. We were descending a long gravel stretch when Mimi jolted to avoid a pothole and Pearl bucked her off. The injuries were brutal: a concussion, a broken collarbone, cracked ribs, a puncture wound in her side, and a broken thumb. When she came to, she did what only Mimi would do; she calmly directed her own care like the ICU nurse she is, while Tara and I waited for the Garmin inReach® SOS to be answered.

A young man in a big truck stopped and loaded all three bikes and all our gear into his truck. He then drove me into Fernie, British Columbia while Tara traveled with Mimi. The rescuers were kind. The hospital staff was wonderful. Even the hotel owner bought us ice cream because, in his words, it was "critical to healing." By the time we finally stopped moving that night, I felt the full weight of our name, TLC *(Tender Loving Care* and *Three Ladies Cycling)*, in a way I never expected.

Discharge, Logistics, and the Strange Stillness

Day 4 - Saturday, August 20
At a Hotel in Fernie
0 miles today • 94.4 miles total

My little red notebook for the days after the crash was surprisingly blank. No notes. No details. No documentation of dates, times, or progress. That night and the days that followed were both a focus and a blur.

Day four had a surreal quiet to it, the kind that follows adrenaline. Mimi was released from the hospital that morning. The female doctor who discharged her stepped outside to look at our bikes. She was an avid cyclist, and for a few minutes we talked about gear and gravel instead of concussions and cracked ribs.

The rest of the day was logistics wrapped in tenderness. At the bike shop, a young woman packed up Pearl for travel and then arranged for her father to drive Mimi the three hours to the Calgary airport on Sunday night. Tara and I decided to keep most of Mimi's gear to ship home on Monday so she wouldn't have to wrestle with it one-handed.

We wandered the town, ate more ice cream, and lived in that odd stillness of being between chapters—not riding, not yet restarting—just taking care of our friend and absorbing what had happened.

Too Much Joie de Vivre?

Afterward, Mimi said, "Maybe I had too much *joie de vivre*." That comment lodged itself in my mind for days. Could joy really be excessive? Could it cause calamity? Would my own *joie de vivre,* my daily ritual of opening the door and saying to the universe, "good morning world," my relentless positivity, my hamster-on-a-wheel energy, lead me into danger too? Should we all just stay home in our safe little worlds?

Since the crash, I've been contemplating joy and whether you can "have too much." So many of us live fenced-in lives. Some fences we build ourselves, to protect our delicate egos, to keep others out, like a garden fence protecting squash from deer. Other fences are handed to us by parents, society, fear. We justify them: feeding the family, saving for retirement, paying for long-term care insurance. (When did that become a priority? Take me out back and shoot me.)

Some people truly love their jobs. Many more pine for what could have been, if only they had dared.

To me, *joie de vivre* is that elusive emotion when you physically feel the door to your heart opening and a sunbeam streaming out. Warmth. Elation. Love. Accomplishment. Wonder. Relief. A thousand emotions, but always an outpouring. I've felt it many times, more frequently now that I'm pursuing my passions and no longer working in corporate America. Sometimes it's fleeting, a beaming moment of joy or relief. Sometimes it's monumental: earning a degree, completing a marathon, passing a certification exam, successfully completing a search and rescue mission. Each time, the shutters of the heart swing open. And then, eventually, they close again. The light filters through the slats. And then even the slats close. In minutes or days, you return to a new "normal," the ecstatic joy tucked safely away.

Other times, joy is simple. Playing cards with my mom and sisters each week, laughing through lunch, always trying to beat Mom, who can count five decks. Those days bring a quieter *joie de vivre*, like colorful sunbeams filtered through stained glass windows.

I love people who live life loudly, lovingly, bravely being themselves. Annie with the pink boa. Roger with the brain implant for Parkinson's, extending his ability to stay active. Nancy, who claims she's boring but is the most directly honest person I know. Angie at the bank with the huge smile that lights up her eyes. Julie, whom I liked instantly, who exudes friendly, happy energy. These beautiful souls have an abundance of *joie de vivre*, and my heart sings when I see them.

I don't think Mimi had too much *joie de vivre*. It didn't cause the crash. As someone who spends a lot of time adventuring, I can tell you: sometimes shit happens. She dared to live her dream. The crash was a crash, nothing more. Her joy didn't cause it. More joy is needed in this world—to bring light to others and to live by example.

One can never have too much *joie de vivre.*

Coffee, Conversations, and Accepting the Restart

Day 5 – Sunday, August 21
8.5 miles today • 102.9 miles total
At a Hotel in Fernie

Sunday morning was slow and gentle. We sat with coffees and talked with Mimi about the trip, about her flight, about the plan to ship her gear home. She was bruised and bandaged and still somehow the most positive person at the table. There was a quiet acceptance in the air.

Mimi called home to update her family and friends, making the personal arrangements that come with an abrupt end to an adventure. She handled it with her usual calm, even though she was injured and facing surgery. Listening to her steady voice as she reassured everyone made the whole situation feel both real and unreal at the same time.

While she made her calls, Tara and I took our unloaded bikes out for a short spin on the local trails. The bikes felt unnervingly light, almost insubstantial, after just three days of hauling full gear. My legs didn't quite trust it. The ease felt wrong, like we'd forgotten something essential. And of course, we had. Mimi wasn't with us.

The trail was beautiful, but there was an ache threaded through it. I kept glancing over my shoulder out of habit, expecting to see her behind me or ahead of me or stopped to take a picture. Instead, it was just the two of us, pedaling through a quiet that didn't feel earned. It was the first time I understood, in my body, that TLC - Three Ladies Cycling—had already shifted into something else.

We rode only long enough to shake out our nerves, then coasted back into town. Mimi was still on the phone, still smiling, still somehow the emotional ballast of the group even while injured. By afternoon, the day had settled into acceptance. She would fly home. We would restart tomorrow. And the trip, whether we liked it or not, had entered its next chapter.

We all knew the trip had split into a before and after, and Sunday was the hinge.

Tara and I would restart on Monday. Mimi would head back to Boston. TLC - Three Ladies Cycling – had become Two Ladies Cycling, a somber shift for all of us.

Me

When I think about our trio, I always picture motion. Tara moves like an engine, reliable, powerful, impossible to stop. Mimi moves like a swan-boat, graceful, buoyant, propelled by a quiet strength that sneaks up on you. And then there's me, the engineer in the middle, trying to keep pace with both the engine and the swan while making sure we're still on the trail and I've packed the right snacks. Someone must keep the system running.

I'm happiest with a plan, a list, and a backup list tucked out of sight but accessible. I like knowing where the next water source is, how many miles remain, and what time the sun sets. Give me a map and a highlighter and I'm content. Give me a steep climb next to Tara and I'm still willing, just maybe questioning my training choices and wondering why my legs didn't get the same factory settings as hers.

Movement has always been my native language: running, hiking, biking, backpacking, kayaking, and now bikepacking. I thrive in nature, even if I sometimes arrive undertrained and overly optimistic. I'm not the strongest rider, especially beside Tara, who seems to have been engineered in a different facility altogether. And Mimi brings a lightness that softens even the hardest days. Between the two of them, I find my own rhythm—somewhere between power and play.

My strength shows up differently. I'm the planner, the organizer, the one who anticipates needs and quietly keeps things on track. I solve problems with an engineer's clarity and a distance runner's stubbornness. I'm practical, persistent, and not easily rattled, unless emotions sneak up on me, which they sometimes do, like the day we waited for the SAR helicopter. Gratitude, humiliation, relief. I'm still not sure which one hit first, but they all arrived uninvited and right on top of each other.

Out on the trail, I'm the grounding force. I bring order without dampening the adventure, structure without rigidity. I keep us oriented, prepared, and moving forward, even when the climb is steep and Tara is already around the bend.

Together, we make an unlikely but perfect trio. Tara brings the power, Mimi brings the buoyancy, and I bring the structure. Tara keeps us moving; Mimi keeps us laughing; I keep us pointed in the right direction. It's a rhythm that works—solid, buoyant, grounded.

When Mimi crashed and had to step out of the trek, the shift was subtle but unmistakable. The pace naturally picked up under Tara's faster rhythm, and I found myself missing the gentle balance Mimi brought. She had a way of softening the hard edges of a day, of turning strain into something almost playful. Without her, the trail felt a little more serious, a little less sparkly. I hadn't realized how much her presence steadied me in its own way.

Still, Tara and I carried on, as we always do, she with her quiet competence, me with my lists and determination. But I felt the absence of Mimi's laughter, her mischief, her ability to make even the grueling parts feel like a shared joke. The trio had become a duo, and the rhythm changed.

What remains, though, is the truth of who we are. Tara, with her red braids and unstoppable strength. Mimi, with her swan-boat grace and sparkling eyes. And me, the analytical one, the planner, the middle note between power and play.

Three different kinds of motion. Three different kinds of strength. And somehow, when we're together, it all works. Yet now we are no longer all together. Will this change our dynamics? Are we less strong without our third team member?

When the Bridge Is Washed Out, Turn Around

Day 6 - Monday, August 22
35 miles today • 137.9 miles total
To Baynes Lake RV Park

Mondays are for starting over. We woke without Mimi this morning, and the absence was immediate, like a three-legged stool trying to remember how to stand. We packed up our room, sorted gear, and boxed up Mimi's things along with a few of our own "what were we thinking" items. Then we waited for the post office to open, balancing boxes on our bike seats and pushing our loaded bikes through the town of Fernie, tipping and teetering like practicing a new circus act.

The morning sun was spectacular. We passed the Tower of the Holy Family Catholic Church and the 1911 granite courthouse, landmarks we somehow missed earlier. The church tower glowed with backlit drama, mountains rising behind it like they were auditioning for a postcard. Fernie is surrounded by so many peaks I've stopped trying to identify any of them.

Tara managed to shed about five pounds of gear. I, however, was thwarted by my own honesty. I couldn't bring myself to tell the postal clerk that my lithium battery light was not a lithium battery light, so I had to keep it. Same with the heavy charger. Heavy weight I had decided I did not need, still to be weighing on me with every pedal stroke. But I didn't want to be responsible for a postal truck fire. We're taking risks on this trip, but not with breaching my integrity. Not yet anyway. So, I ditched a down jacket, a chair (!), and a few other things that sparked less moral conflict. We were now a different TLC—two ladies cycling.

We rode 32 miles to Baynes Lake and camped at an RV park where we felt reasonably safe from BEARS, capital letters entirely appropriate. The trails out of Fernie were smooth singletrack switchbacks, fun and flowy. Yesterday we'd ridden some of them without all the gear on our bikes, and the bikes felt light and lively. Today, fully loaded again, they felt like reluctant pack mules.

Two hours in, we reached a washed-out bridge and a ravine that looked like it had been deeply scoured by a flash flood, because it had. A couple miles earlier there had been a sign warning us about a bridge closure, but we'd chosen optimism over literacy. *Closure* was an interesting choice of words, as opposed to *missing*. My "push on at all costs" instinct was still overpowering my common sense, which was trying to tap me on the shoulder and whisper, *not this time.*

Backtracking meant going uphill, which I loathe, and the noticeable weight compared to yesterday was heavy on my mind. The truth is, my resistance to turning around didn't start on this trip. That habit was forged decades earlier, in my first engineering job, where turning around was never an option, even if it should have been.

I didn't understand it then, but that job taught me a lot about stubbornness, and even more about survival.

> I was the first female engineer in the paper mill, which meant I was expected to knock before entering the production office, a rule that applied only to me and Paula, the lone female scheduler. No man with a Y chromosome had ever knocked on that door in the history of the mill, but somehow, we were the

ones who needed permission to enter the room where all the real decisions were made. I learned early to swallow my irritation and keep moving. Emotional control was perhaps one of the first engineering skills.

One morning the assistant superintendent, a man who regularly commented on my body as if it were part of the equipment list, told me, "A vendor dropped off donuts at the guard shack, go get them for us."

I didn't even hesitate.

"Fuck you," I said. "Get your own donuts."

I'd grown up with three brothers and a constellation of uncles. I could take it, and I could dish it out. And in that moment, I wasn't about to play the role of office waitress just because I had ovaries.

But I wasn't immune to missteps. Once, after the plant superintendent sprayed me with a hose, part of the mill's charming hazing ritual, I snapped back with a word I'd grown up using with my brothers, never understanding its weight or its harm. He didn't speak to me for two weeks. When I finally asked why, he said, "I have nine grown children. I am not a "fag".

I was stunned. Not because he was offended, but because I had been so naïve. I hadn't understood the context, the history, the hurt, or the interpreted derogatory nature of it. I was a naïve child. That moment became part of my education in the world beyond rural Maine.

And then there was the night in Atlanta, at a Ritz Carlton of all places, when that same superintendent asked if I wanted to "fool around." I said no, for a dozen reasons I didn't bother listing, and we never spoke of it again. He taught me a lot over the years, shared industry knowledge freely, never held a grudge. People are complicated. Mills are complicated. I was young.

All of that lived somewhere in me as I stared at the washed-out bridge, the part of me that used to push forward no matter what, the part that didn't know how to turn around, the part that thought grit meant never backing down.

But today, grit meant something different, and we did not back down.

We took inventory of every rope, bungee, and strap we owned and concocted a plan that would have made a Scout leader weep with pride or concern. Tara scrambled down first, hanging onto an overhanging tree like some kind of red-haired mountain lemur. She declared the descent "doable," which is Taraspeak for "marginally insane but survivable."

We removed all the panniers and I handed them down, then lowered the bikes one at a time using our daisy-chained straps. It was ridiculous, and at the time, I posted the video on my blog because it was too crazy not to share.

It took about an hour, including a quick lunch, to get everything down and back up the other side. Tara muscled her bike up alone. I needed her to haul mine from above while I pushed from behind, which felt like the world's slowest, sweatiest team-building exercise. But we did it. Safely. And safety is very much top-of-mind these days, with Mimi continually in our thoughts.

As we sat catching our breath, we heard a pack of dogs barreling toward us, barking like they'd been hired for dramatic effect. A lone cyclist joined them, and corralled them, heading back down the way they had come.

When we reached the *next* washed-out bridge, we didn't even pretend to consider crossing. We saw the sign, consulted the map, and immediately found a detour. We chalked that learning up to serious personal growth, proof you can teach old ladies new tricks.

The detour took us past a major pipeline construction project, lots of heavy equipment, and what looked like a firefighting staging camp. We've been checking fire-tracking websites regularly—another new habit born of this trip.

Later, we cooled off in the Elk River, then found a gas station where we filled our water bottles with slushies. Tara has an addiction to purple slushies. We also bought chips and jellybeans, but let's keep that between us. My health-conscious sister Angela doesn't need to know my desperate fueling sources.

The final stretch was pavement with chaotic traffic, then a sweep of dry grassland that looked almost prairie-like. The air felt hotter, the landscape significantly drier. Mimi texted saying she'd landed safely in Boston and would see a hand surgeon tomorrow. We already missed her humor and giggles; the silence was noticeable.

By 9:30 p.m., the temperature was still in the 80s. We were tired, dusty, and proud. It was a strong day back on the trail—and a reminder that sometimes the bravest thing you can do is turn around.

Chapter 4: The Unexpected Gift of Finding My People

Tara introduced me to the song *Find Your People* by Drew Holcomb & The Neighbors and it resonated with me. I now recognize new tribe members early on in relationships.

The song is about the rare kind of friends who steady you when the world tilts, the ones who see who you are before you've said a word. It celebrates the people who call your bluff with love, who walk beside you when the road turns rough, who understand your quirks and your silences, and who hold you to your best self. Its message is simple and generous: when you find the people who lift you up instead of weighing you down, you don't just feel supported, you start to recognize yourself more clearly in their reflection. These are your people and are to be treasured.

Scatdaddling

Day 7 - Tuesday, August 23
46.5 miles today • 184.4 miles total
To Dickey Lake State Park

Every morning begins with the ritual of weighmetry, our made-up term for symmetry, but with weight. The panniers must be perfectly balanced, so the bikes don't list to one side like drunken pack animals. It's a small ceremony of order before the chaos of the trail, a moment where everything is briefly aligned, as generally Tara and I are also.

We left Baynes Lake RV Park sometime before 8:30 a.m., after the usual two-hour routine of coffee, breakfast, breaking down camp, and packing the bikes. Coyotes had yipped and yapped through the night, a soundtrack that felt oddly familiar, like home, but wilder. Their excitement over dinner was palpable. I get it.

At the Roosville border crossing, the guard asked where we were headed. Tara answered "Eureka," which was fourteen miles away. I answered "Mexico," which was twenty-five hundred miles away. Tara understated as always. Me, leaning toward braggadocious. The guard smiled, said "Welcome home," and waved us through.

Just before the border, at a gas station, we met Jon and Lois, former Brits, now Canadians, on fully loaded mountain bikes. They'd ridden from Rossland, BC, to Banff before even starting the Great Divide, adding 500 kilometers to an already massive, planned undertaking. Understated, unassuming, resourceful, gritty. We swapped trail intel and toggled between kilometers and miles, Celsius and Fahrenheit, like a multilingual math club. We liked them immediately and as we rode away, we hoped we would cross paths again.

The day's ride was mostly roads with endless prairie views, amber waves of grain, literally. We stopped for lunch at Subway, resupplied at the grocery store, and checked trail conditions at the forest service office. Another major section of the trail was closed all the way to Wurtz Cabin, so we'd need to reroute. We'd miss some beautiful terrain, but it nudged us ahead of schedule.

We took Tobacco Road, Meadow Creek Road, and Ant Flats Road to Trego, avoiding the highway. Eventually we reached a forest service campground on Dickey Lake. Along the way we rode on Grizzly Bear Path Road, which felt appropriately named given the recent abundance of bear poo. It rained exactly ten drops, just enough to make us put on rain jackets and then immediately regret it. Inside our jackets it was a sauna.

At the campground we reunited with Jon and Lois and met Helen, an older woman from New Zealand riding north-bound alone, having just completed a solo bike trip in Alaska. Another very impressive individual, alone, female, and with a "can-do" attitude. And older. What I aspire to be: an even older woman, still adventuring. She had a nasty gash on her leg from a fall, which she'd treated with honey for its antibacterial properties. We all camped on one site, at a cost of $3 each—a bikepacker's budget.

Jon and Lois told us they were on a one-year hiatus from "traditional life," eventually heading to South America. I admired their bravery and their willingness to live an entire year by pedal stroke. It made our ten-week trek seem less ambitious. I was envious. But I, too, am out here, living my dream, living the me I am learning to be.

Somewhere in the quiet miles that afternoon, my mind drifted back to a job interview early in my career—the one where I spent eight hours being tested, evaluated, and wired up like a lab rat. IQ tests, stress tests, creativity tests. I called it my "psych evaluation," and I'm still not convinced half of it was legal.

At the end of the day, the evaluators told me, "You don't quit. You keep trying in the face of impossibility, and you are incredibly creative."

I accept that I am too stubborn to quit, but creative? Me?

At the time, I thought creativity belonged to painters and sculptors, not engineers who counted backwards by sevens while hooked up to electrodes. My definition of creativity was narrow enough that I never saw myself inside it. In retrospect, it was just another sign of how naïve I was, hungry for every job opportunity, desperate to prove myself, and convinced that effort alone could shape a life.

It shifted my mindset and redefined creativity for me. I am definitely a problem solver, creative in ways to survive, thrive, move forward. That re-understanding was again confirmed on this trail. Creativity isn't just about art. It's about adaptation. It's about finding a way forward when the path disappears. It's about refusing to quit when the climb gets steep. Out here, creativity is survival. And maybe I've had more of it than I ever gave myself credit for.

We swam in the lake, doubling the dip as both a bath and a laundry cycle. Helen seemed irritated that Tara and I did everything together, swimming, cooking, organizing. We're both naturally cooperative and kind, but she seemed to interpret it as a lack of independence. Funny how quickly people judge based on their own expectations. Perhaps her sharp criticism of our "togetherness" explains why she was traveling alone.

As we rode, we invented more bicycle-touring vocabulary. Yesterday's word had been *weighmetry*. Today's word was *scatdaddle*, a combination of scat and skedaddle. Defined as: to depart quickly upon spotting multiple piles of bear poo. We had seen tall piles, flat piles, long trails of Hershey-squirt piles spaced evenly for fifty feet, all full of berries. We scatdaddled all day. I hadn't taken photos when the concept was new, but I finally captured a big pile yesterday for posterity.

It was a long, full, satisfying day—new country, new friends, new words, and a growing sense that this adventure was expanding in ways we couldn't have predicted.

In hindsight, it was the day we began to find our people. The ones who would ride with us for the next two months. The ones who made the road feel less lonely. The ones who reminded me of something I'd been slow to learn: You can't go it alone. Not in wind. Not in waves. Not in life. Turns out the same is true on a bike.

Finding My People

I didn't know I was searching for a tribe until the first time I trudged down a mountain in the dark, a stretcher pulling on the strap over my shoulder, breath fogging the cold air. Search and Rescue (SAR) wasn't glamorous—most of it was mud, sweat, and the metallic smell of adrenaline—but it was the first place where my heartbeat matched the rhythm of the people around me. We hiked through sleet and silence, swapping dinner ideas as if we weren't carrying someone's worst day between us. In SAR, I found my people. I found where I belonged and felt I could contribute to society.

Before that, I kept trying to give back in ways that never quite fit. I was a Girl Scout assistant leader for a while, then tried the Boy Scout program. I believed in service, in showing up, in being useful. But the truth was, I was better at tying knots than managing preteen chaos. When I volunteered with Girls on the Run, I learned quickly that I was not built for the emotional weather systems of preadolescent girls. The teachers I coached with deserved Olympic medals for their ability to redirect meltdowns with a single raised eyebrow.

"They are not my people," Tara once told me. She worked in a city hospital, surrounded by coworkers who talked about parties, makeup, new restaurants, and the latest movies. She loved them, she said, but they weren't her people. On Friday nights, while they slipped into heels and lipstick, Tara drove north toward her yurt in the New Hampshire mountains. She skied, hiked, pedaled gravel roads until her legs hummed. She wore no makeup. She went to bed by eight. She was, in every way, a creature of the woods. And between us, we had found more of our tribe.

I understood her. Some of us are built for fluorescent lights and small talk; others need the hush of pines and the honest work of cold hands. Some find belonging in break rooms; others find it on switchbacks.

For me, belonging arrived with the weight of a stretcher and the steady footsteps of people who moved through the world the way I did—physically, purposefully, with a kind of shared grit. I didn't have to explain myself. I didn't have to pretend. I just had to show up, boots laced, headlamp ready.

And that was enough.

Detours and TLC of Our Bikes

Day 8 - Wednesday, August 24
45.3 miles today • 229.7 miles total
To Whitefish Lake State Park

Thunderstorms hammered us through the night, and by morning everything we owned was soaked. The tents sagged with water weight, my personal nemesis, and every movement sent cold droplets down our necks. Wet tents suck. They're heavy, demoralizing, and make me question every ounce I've chosen to carry.

As if the damp wasn't enough, the logging trucks started before dawn. Beep. Beep. Beep. A soundtrack I know well, though I still can't fathom why every machine this morning seems to run in reverse more than it drives forward.

We shook out what water we could and packed up, the added weight pressing on my psyche more than on the bike. A construction closure forced us onto a detour up Stryker Whitefish Road, fifteen miles to reconnect with the route, ten of them a slow grind. Up and up and up. But the cool, overcast morning helped, and both Tara and I felt strong.

Three hours in, we stopped for lunch beside a gated side road. My legs were humming, my brain drifting, and between bites of whatever-passed-for-lunch, I realized the effort I was pouring into this adventure felt a lot like earning my first college degree. The climb had that same flavor: uncertainty, wrong turns, quiet panic, and the stubborn refusal to quit. It reminded me of being nineteen and wildly unprepared for the thing I'd signed up for and somehow doing it anyway.

> I didn't fully comprehend the challenges ahead of us on this adventure. But then again, I didn't fully comprehend college either, and I made it through that. "Lucky" isn't the right word for making it to graduation (or to the start of this trip), but I certainly benefitted from family support and a refusal to quit, even after scoring a glorious five on my first chemistry exam. A single digit. A number better suited to golf than academics. Later in life, a hiring manager would politely rebrand this trait as "perseverance and tenacity," which sounded much better than "too stubborn to quit even when the data suggested otherwise."
>
> In the days leading up to graduation, I had my first real epiphany: I was truly going to earn a Bachelor of Science in Chemical Engineering. Me, the girl who coasted through high school on natural ability and zero study habits. It turns out you really can do almost anything with enough persistence, panic, and late-night problem sets.

My family didn't come from a long line of college graduates. My parents are smart and capable—simply shaped by the world they grew up in. They were experts in their environment. Mom could count cards, balance a checkbook to the penny, and whip up a meal for ten in thirty minutes. Dad built TVs and ham radios, and was one of the first to take a class on fiber optics. We were classic rural Mainers—never lacking intelligence, just exposure. Environment shapes us more than we realize, especially when you grow up far from anything resembling a city.

I was living in a rickety third-floor apartment north of campus, the kind of place where the floor slanted just enough to make you question your inner ear, when it hit me: I was going to graduate. The surge of emotion I felt then was stronger than anything I felt on graduation day itself. Maybe because on graduation day I was too busy sweating in polyester robes and trying not to trip.

Getting there had not been easy. My high school chemistry teacher had bragged endlessly about how well-prepared his students were. I believed him. Then I failed my first college chemistry exam. I had no study habits, no systems, and no clue. I was also taking calculus, physics, and an elective, and I arrogantly decided I only had time to study for three of the four. Chemistry drew the short straw.

After that spectacular failure, I went to see the professor, Dr. Goodfriend, a name that turned out to be wildly misleading. He asked me to work a problem on the board. I couldn't. I admitted I hadn't studied and asked whether I could still pass if I worked hard the rest of the semester. His response: "What are you doing here? You don't even know the basics. You'll never make it in Chemical Engineering." Humiliating. Demoralizing. Motivating, in a spite-fueled sort of way. I earned Bs or better on every exam after that and still "only" scraped out a C. I harbored anger about that for years. On reflection and maturity, a victory, considering the circumstances.

I also lost my scholarship after my first year. High school had been too easy, and college hit me like a freight train. I nearly flunked out. When I think about how different my life might have been if I hadn't clawed my way back, it still scares me. But I went back. And toward the end of year two, things clicked. Statics and Strength of Materials, of all classes, turned me around. It was fascinating and I finally learned how to learn. My internship at a paper mill helped too. Suddenly, the equations had real-world meaning, and I was being paid to understand them. A revelation: learning is easier when it is applicable and the bonus is when someone hands you a paycheck.

After graduation, I learned many of my classmates had cheated their way through exams. Meanwhile, I was over here playing by the rules, except in golf, where I freely admit I don't keep score properly, but at least I'm transparent about it. Apparently, during exams, students would flip completed pages facedown so the next person could "borrow" their work. My score of thirty-nine on one exam was scaled to a B. I still don't understand how a professor can feel good about an exam where the average score requires life support.

One of my roommates, the valedictorian and the person who always ruined the curve for the rest of us, left school for a few months during senior year. The pressure had gotten to her, and she couldn't show up for interviews. She was brilliant but paralyzed by perfection. I can still see her handwriting, calculating my share of the phone bill, carried out to four decimal places. I was stunned. College had been hard for me too, and I'd doubted myself plenty, but I'd pushed through. Somehow, I made it and the interviews were the whole point.

And that's the through-line—college, this adventure, the whole messy middle. I wasn't the strongest or the fastest, and I sure didn't start out as the academic standout. But I am persistent. Stubborn. Tenacious. The kind of person who can tank an exam, refuse to quit, and grind her way to an engineering degree anyway. Honestly, that might be the credential that means the most to me.

And, with all the planning, training, and persistence, I had graduated to the trail.

Existential crisis complete, lunch consumed, legs still attached—it was time to get back on the bike.

After lunch, the descent began—down, down, down. I love going down. My mind, however, is a trickster: confident in my ability yet whining about the effort I'll need to expend later. Why complain when I'm here by choice?

We rejoined the Great Divide near Upper Whitefish Lake. In five or six hours of riding, we saw only three cars and three cyclists. The approach into Whitefish was dramatic, riding high above the lake with a steep drop to our right, no guardrails, and fully loaded bikes that felt just a bit too top-heavy for comfort. But the pavement made for a glorious glide into town.

At Whitefish Lake State Park, we reunited with Jon and Louis and met a Danish couple cycling from Alaska to South America. As intimidating as our adventure feels, theirs dwarfs it. Alaska to South America is a lot of miles.

Tonight before bed, Tara spend time cleaning up a dinner spill with the seriousness of a hazmat technician, our nightly ritual of bear-prevention TLC.

Nice Hat, Jen

Day 9 - Thursday, August 25
40.1 miles today • 269.8 miles total
To Bigfork State Park

Exhaustion is catching up with me. I accidentally posted my daily blog summary twice—my brain apparently running on the fumes left over after my muscles took their share. Freight trains chugged and tooted through the night, and thunderstorms rolled through again. Sleep was intermittent.

We packed up early and headed straight to the Buffalo Café for a BIG breakfast. Hot food is rocket fuel.

Much of the day was riding on pavement. We stopped at a retired train engine in Columbia Falls, conveniently equipped with a porta-potty, and then rolled through farmland: hayfields, fenced gardens, and deer. So many deer. One tiny fawn was trapped inside a tall fence, and we felt helpless watching it pace.

The valley was beautiful, framed by tall mountains and dotted with dilapidated farmhouses, scenic and sad at the same time. Abandoned dreams. Children leaving the farms for city lives. I prefer rural, where no one pretends to be anything other than what they are.

Near Bigfork, a gravel bike path carried us the final two miles. No big forks in sight, despite the name. Our campsite at Flathead Lake had what Tara dubbed a "tent litter box"—a gravel-filled rectangle that drained beautifully during the brief thunderstorm that rolled through. After swimming, which again served the dual purpose of bathing and laundry, we rode into town for groceries and Dairy Queen. Almost heaven.

The "nice hat" reference? I stuck my head into a giant hanging flower basket and emerged with what looked like purple hair.

Team Training as a Tea Bag

Day 10 - Friday, August 26
37.5 miles today • 307.3 miles total
To Cedar Creek Remote Site

I finally slept well in the tent litter box. Who knew gravel could be so comforting?

We ended the day at Cedar Creek, south of Flathead Lake. The designated campsite was a swamp, standing puddles, mud, and one small dry rise already occupied. With few options, we camped on the sandy riverbank near the boat launch, right beside a "no camping here" sign. Tara was uneasy about the rule-breaking, but the rising puddles made our choice feel justified. We set up quickly and dove into our tents just as another thunderstorm unleashed itself. The wind was wild but brief. Two young men fished until dark.

We arrived by 3:30 p.m., our now-familiar rhythm: ride early, arrive early, unpack, swim, eat, sleep, repeat.

The day's ride began by back-tracking on the smooth dirt path, then pavement back to Ferndale to reconnect with the route. A long flat stretch led to the big climb, eight or nine miles of gradual ascent. I stopped to adjust my cleat to ease some knee pain. We followed the west side of Swan Lake to the point where we had to choose, to detour to avoid logging trucks or stay on the main route. We chose the main route and saw zero trucks. Our lucky day?

Six riders converged at the same intersection for lunch, which is a rarity. Tara and I had just descended a big hill and been caught in a three-minute rain burst. By the time we reached the others, they hadn't felt a single drop. Weather is fickle out here.

The campsite was 0.8 miles off the trail, all downhill. At the end of the day, that means only one thing: tomorrow starts with a climb. My tired mind dreads it, but the uphill will warm us. And today's cool, overcast weather made for beautiful riding.

> And this is where the reflection comes in, the part I didn't understand then, but do now, as we linked up with Jon and Lois and began to form a stronger team.
>
> Meeting them reminded me of my sea-kayak-guide training back in Maine. That course was the opposite of independence; it was about learning how to read water, weather, and people. It was about knowing when to lead and when to follow. It was about trusting your team enough to let them rescue you if things went sideways.
>
> At one point I served as the class "tea bag"—the designated test dummy who, on command and at the most inconvenient moments, dumped over in my kayak and floated upside-down until the students executed a proper rescue. Humbling, ridiculous, and oddly liberating. You learn a lot about yourself when your job is to tip over on purpose and trust a group of near-strangers to haul you back into your boat.

I'd spent years thinking competence meant doing everything alone, muscling through, proving myself. But guiding taught me something different: real strength is shared. Real safety is communal. Real adventure is rarely a solo act.

Looking back, I can see how that training shaped the way I recognized Jon and Lois as team mates so quickly. They were my kind of people, capable, humble, quietly fierce. The kind you want beside you when the wind shifts or the current turns. The kind who make the hard days feel possible.

Happy 34th Anniversary, John!

Day 11 - Saturday, August 27
40.5 miles today • 347.8 miles total
To Holland Lake Campground

I'm fortunate that John supports my adventures. Secretly, he's probably happy to be rid of me for a while. Another anniversary apart. Absence makes the heart grow fonder or helps to create longevity in a marriage. Whichever it is, it seems to work for us.

It was another wet, soggy morning. Breakfast was, predictably, oatmeal. Fortunately, I like oatmeal. I also eat it when I'm home, generally for second breakfast.

We've taken to rating each bathroom facility, a.k.a. "outhouse." Today's scored a solid "2" on our 1–10 scale. Anything below a "3" warrants pooping in the woods. This one was rickety, spider-filled, filthy, and barely had a path to the broken-down door. It barely warranted a lowly "2". I am not sure what could be worse to warrant a "1".

We waited for the sun to dry our tents a bit before packing up. Nothing lifts my spirits like sunshine and a tent that weighs less than a soaked wool blanket. The 0.8-mile warmup back to the GDMBR trail wasn't as bad as expected; last night's descent had seemed steeper than it really was.

We rode with Jon and Louis today. It was nice to have company, especially theirs. Almost all the miles were on dirt roads: one long climb early, then a mix of up and down. With our food supplies running low, the bikes felt a bit lighter.

We passed Peck Lake, which had been an alternative site for last night's campsite. We were all relieved we hadn't pushed on to this spot, as getting caught in that storm would've been miserable.

Holland Lake Campground was lovely, though our fantasy of ice cream or lodge food evaporated quickly when we walked in and were greeted with indifference. No snacks, essentially no service. Not a bikepacking dream stop. We connected again with Sandra (Germany) and Steve (Montana), who were also camping there. Everyone bathed in the lake, which was a brilliant, almost surreal green.

By 4 p.m. the sky turned overcast and dark. We shared the campsite fee—another cheap night. No cell service to call John on our anniversary, but our Garmin InReach® Mini could send a pre-typed message, so at least he knew we were still alive.

At the time, the day felt straightforward: wet morning, steady miles, good company, disappointing lodge, beautiful lake. But later, when I looked back on it, I realized it carried a familiar thread, the quiet comfort of moving with a group, of falling into a rhythm with people you trust, of knowing your place in the line.

It reminded me of my very first cross-country race in high school. It was the fall of 1979. I didn't think of it on the trail—I was too busy pedaling and trying to stay warm—but the connection surfaced afterward, when I tried to understand why this day stayed with me.

Back then, I'd never been part of a team before. We took a bus to a golf course in Rockland, Maine. The assistant coach told me, "Stay behind Cecelia." Maybe he said, "Stick with Cecelia." Either way, I took it literally. Near the end of the race, the trail turned left and Cecelia kept running straight. I stopped at the junction and yelled, "The trail goes THIS way!" Then I waited for her to come back so she could resume her place in front of me. We finished that way: Cecelia, then me.

Afterward, the coach demanded, "What were you doing?"

"I stayed behind Cecelia like you told me to," I said, genuinely confused.

I laugh about it now—how literal I was, how loyal, how determined to follow instructions even when they made no sense. Today, I love competition and the razzing that comes with it. I'll tell a friend I'm going to "kick their butt" even when I know I'll be trailing behind them the whole way. I don't care about winning. I care about the camaraderie, the shared effort, the joy of moving through the world together.

And that's what Day 11 was: steady miles with good people, the comfort of a small moving tribe, the quiet satisfaction of knowing exactly where I fit in the line.

Today was one more loop. One more mile. One more quiet reminder that I can do this.

All is well.

I love Pizza

Day 12 - Sunday, August 28
35.2 miles today, + 6–7 town miles • 383 miles total
To Seeley Lake

We left Holland Lake around 8:30 a.m. and climbed steadily until lunchtime. Despite the elevation gain, it felt like a short day because we knew we'd end in a town with services—hot food, laundry, showers, and the promise of feeling human again.

Mornings on the bike pass quickly; afternoons tend to drag, especially when I'm tired.

The Seeley Lake campground was about three miles before the downtown and services, so we went to the campground and set up camp first. We expected to pay $5 for the group, but another cyclist, Dan from Wisconsin, arrived with only a $20. No one had change, so he paid for everyone. Trail magic. Thanks, Dan.

Then came the logistical puzzle: which order? Takeout, laundry, and showers? Which was the most needed? We decided laundry, then showers, then food. We discovered that the laundromat had showers, so exciting for me to consider the efficiency of this! But the showers required a mountain of quarters, and the sign instructed us to go to the local bar for change. We thought, "well, this should be interesting!"

Tara headed across the parking lot to the bar while I loaded the laundry. The showers, tucked in the back of the laundromat, were sketchy, but stinky people can't be choosy. The Seeley Lake campground had pit toilets and no showers, and the lake was too cold for a swim, so a laundromat shower felt luxurious and efficient. Showering while the clothes washed checked two things off the list simultaneously. A good, strong dopamine hit for me!

Then, PIZZA. I was so happy.

And maybe because it was the day after our anniversary, or maybe because I was tired and hungry and finally clean, but eating pizza cracked open a small door in my mind.

Somewhere in the middle of our marriage, my mind finally stopped arguing with my heart about food. For years I'd overridden what I liked and wanted in favor of what I thought I should like, healthier, cleaner, more virtuous. I'm not holier than thou, though I fear I sometimes come across that way. But somewhere along the miles, on bikes, on foot, in life, I finally admitted the truth: I liked what John liked. I didn't need to suggest a salad to prove anything. For us, that thing was pizza.

One year I tracked how much we spent on it, over $480, almost all from Porfido's Market. Once a week, like clockwork, we'd pick up a $9.99 pepperoni pizza because our lives were too full to cook every night. We were biking after work, building our house, seeing friends. A weekly pizza wasn't indulgence; it felt lazy but was survival. It was also consistency, one of the quiet stabilizers of a long marriage.

Before John moved to our cottage in Maine, I convinced him to switch to broccoli pizza from the competitive market across the street, Gold House. I told myself it was healthier and

I preferred variety, and maybe it met those desires, but the minute he moved to Maine, I switched right back to pepperoni from Porfido's. It's funny how you feel influenced in a marriage without realizing it. Only when the influence is gone do you see the comfort it provided. The ritual. The ease. The way small, predictable things help you weather the rough spots.

So yes—pizza in a dive near the laundromat, after a sketchy shower and a long day on the bike, tasted like home. Like marriage. Like the kind of love that doesn't need candles or anniversaries or grand gestures. Just something warm, familiar, and exactly what you really want.

We talked to Mimi while eating our pizza (her hand surgery went well), then rode the miles back to camp. Food is always a balancing act—enough calories without too much weight. The lake was beautiful as the sun set and the temperature dropped.

In the campground, deer wandered everywhere, including several spotted fawns. I finally spoke to John and wished him a proper Happy Anniversary. We've probably spent more anniversaries apart than together in our thirty-four years, and we're both fine with that. We're terrible at celebrating, and in some low-pressure way, we like it.

Jon was up sick in the night—burgers gone wrong. Or maybe it was the half gallon of milk he drank. Feeling bad on a bike trip while camping is misery.

Chapter 5: Where the Trail Gets Real

My Gap

A flaw of my striving personality is that I've read every happiness book ever written. If there were loyalty points for self-help, I'd have earned a free upgrade to Enlightenment Class by now. I make resolutions. I tape goals to mirrors. I buy the next book. I am, in short, a self-improvement junkie, always in pursuit of that elusive emotion.

I'd like to think I've outgrown it, but even now, reading *Breath* by James Nestor, I'm still trying to optimize myself into serenity.

When I turned fifty, one of those books, and a well-meaning friend, told me I needed to "reduce my GAP." The GAP, they explained, is the distance between where you spend your time and where you *wish* you spent your time. A simple concept:

- Make a list of things that make you happy.
- Make a list of things you do every day.
- Compare the lists.
- Adjust accordingly.

My "happy list" was easy: being outside, being active, spending time with friends and family, reading, working in the yard with John.

My "daily list" was also easy: work, work, work, work, work.

The GAP wasn't subtle. It was less a gap and more the Grand Canyon, carved over decades of striving, responsibility, and the belief that productivity was the rent I paid for existing. And the worst part? I'd been living this pattern my entire adult life, convinced that if I just kept going, it would eventually feel right.

The point wasn't the lists. It was that I had spent my entire adult life trying to escape work and reach the life I believed I was meant for, a life outside, a life in motion, a life that felt like adventure instead of obligation. The GAP exercise didn't reveal anything new; it simply documented a truth I'd been dodging for decades. I wasn't living the life I wanted. I was managing the life I had built and dreaming of the one just beyond it.

By all external measures, I should have been happy. I was healthy, fit, reasonably athletic. I had a "good job" and had stayed employed through the recession. I had a husband who loves animals, babies, the elderly, and me with equal tenderness. He is passionate and kind. I am... emotionally even-keeled. Let's call it that.

I'm not much of a celebrator, and I don't complain often—unless the topic is work. Despite my commitment, I never felt that I truly loved any of my nine jobs. Where was my passion? I was always scanning the horizon for a trailhead, a bike route, a way outside. I used to marvel at people who stayed in one field for thirty years, becoming experts in a single sliver of the world. That was never my path. Maybe that's my "pain body," as the spiritual teachers call it—a lifelong itch of professional restlessness.

I am a striver. First daughter, third of six kids. I spent my childhood trying to compensate for my older brothers' teenage chaos by being the Responsible One. I strove. I excelled. I unintentionally collected job titles like some people collect souvenir shot glasses. Reinventing as needed.

As a chemical engineering graduate with a paper science concentration (yes, that was a real thing) I entered an industry that barely exists now. But I did some genuinely interesting things. I helped make the first prototype watermarked U.S. currency, which led to an interview with the CIA. I ran a toilet paper converting facility. I made brown hand towels. I once shipped a truckload of hand towels that did not meet specifications and would not dispense, a mistake I did not repeat. And for the record, toilet paper should not contain wet-strength chemicals, unless you want to clog the Atlanta Airport bathrooms. That one was not error.

I helped stabilize a start-up food co-op. I worked as a commercial loan officer. At 50 years old, I was the Director of Sales Operations for a pharmaceutical manufacturing company. And yet, despite all this, I never felt true job satisfaction. My heart has always been elsewhere, usually outside, preferably near water, ideally with a backpack.

I spent years pining for the next adventure trip, the next escape. I was afraid to live the life I felt called to. What life was that? I wasn't sure. Kayak instructor. Botanist. Naturalist in a national park.

All of which pay approximately eight dollars an hour. That might be the root of the fear.

At 48, I went on a vision quest with my friend Becca as my spiritual guide. My big revelation, upon seeing a bird's nest, was: *You can build a home anywhere.* Later, as a hawk circled overhead and I lay in my bright red bivy sack, I jerked awake and said aloud, "I'm not dead." Which felt like a line in the sand, an opportunity to recommit to my life dreams. Maybe I had been a little dead, or at least dormant, for too long.

Then came Barcelona. New Year's Eve. Me and my twenty-year-old niece, lying on our backs in a tiny room, wearing red underwear because tradition says it brings good luck. She was a college student with debt, yet she chose to travel with her aging aunt. I think she is brave. Her parents probably thought she was reckless.

Before midnight, we talked about resolutions. She said, with the kind of confidence that comes from knowing exactly what she wants her life to be, that my resolutions should be:

- Sell the house
- Move to Maine
- Find a new job
- Run a marathon

The young have a refreshing lack of fear and an ability to keep things simple. Why do we, the "responsible adults," carry so much fear? I was negotiating with myself. What did I have to fear?

Since retiring, my GAP has finally begun to shrink. Turns out, when you stop working sixty hours a week, you have time for things like sunlight, hobbies, and noticing that you're still alive.

Maybe that's the real lesson: the GAP doesn't close all at once. It closes one small, brave, seemingly insignificant decision at a time.

Keep the Rubber Side Down

Day 13 - Monday, August 29
48 miles today • 431 miles total

To Big Nelson Forest Service Site

It was cold at Seeley Lake this morning, about 35°F. We followed our familiar routine: wake up, pack the gear, drink coffee, eat breakfast, wait for the tent to dry as much as possible, pack the stove, sort out the day's food, and finally get on the bike. Full gloves, warm tights, jackets. And the sacred ritual of toe warmers: open the packets, shake them awake, stick them to your socks, and slide into your bike shoes. Warm feet guaranteed, even if nothing else is warm.

The ride to Ovando was eventful. Jonathan was still not feeling well after last night's burger and milk extravaganza. He spent part of the night in the pit toilet, an experience no one deserves. Tara and I both could have slept longer, but we're committed to early starts.

Our days often began with a climb, which doubled as a warm, up. I welcomed the uphill; I needed the heat. We stopped every 30–45 minutes for snacks, clothing adjustments, and pee breaks. Mid-morning, we skidded to a stop as a black bear ran up a tree about twenty feet from us. We'd surprised each other, us barreling downhill on gravel, the bear minding its own business. Clinging to the trunk about fifteen feet up, it stared at us while we stared back. It wasn't very big and quickly decided the tree was not the best escape route. It backed down and sprinted up the road.

A few minutes later we stopped again at a shallow, mostly dried-up pond with tracks across it, bear? deer? We were too high on the bank to tell. While fiddling with my phone for a picture, I tipped over. It happens to everyone at some point on a long bike trip. Only the ego bruises.

At the time, I didn't connect any of this, the cold morning, the bear, the tip-over, to anything larger. I was just trying to stay upright and keep moving. But later, when I looked back on this day and tried to understand why it stuck with me, I realized it echoed a familiar pattern in my life: the feeling of charging into the deep, improvising my way through it, and somehow finding a foothold, going along and conforming, to get along.

In my early 30s, I'd been in an MBA class in rural northern New Hampshire. There were only six or seven of us, all working adults. One night the professor announced that someone in the room didn't belong because she hadn't completed the required undergraduate prerequisites. I had almost eight years of hands-on cost accounting experience, but no formal cost accounting class. I raised my hand and said, "That would be me." I can acknowledge my shortcomings. Maybe I didn't belong, but I was going to give it my best.

The professor had a reputation for almost never giving an A. I figured out how to get along: I baked cookies every week. He was a bit portly, and I always needed brain fuel to survive a three-hour class. Sugar helped both of us. On the day of the final exam, I chose studying over baking. When I walked into the classroom, he looked up and said, "Jennifer, where are the cookies?" Oops. I got an A anyway.

I didn't think about that story on the trail, not consciously. But when I look back at day thirteen, I see the same thread running through it: I may not always feel like I belong, but I show up, I work hard, and I find a way. Sometimes it's cookies. Sometimes it's stubbornness. Sometimes it's just getting back on the bike after tipping over.

We rolled into the infamous town of Ovando, beloved by cyclists and known among Great Divide riders for a tragic grizzly attack a few years ago. Tara and I had packages waiting at the post office, both containing Butt Butter or chamois cream, used daily to keep our nether regions lubricated. A long bike trip can become torture with saddle sores so daily maintenance and stops for reapplication were critical, especially on hot days. Tara's package also had food, a sleeping bag liner, and maple candies (a taste of home) from Larry. My box included enough peanut butter crackers to feed a small army. I shared the extras as there was no need to add more weight to my panniers or my psyche.

We spent a couple of hours in town: eating, having ice creams, writing postcards, charging phones, texting. We lounged on the porch of a historic building with power outlets, cyclist gold. Ovando offers quirky lodging options: an old jail cell, a covered wagon, a teepee. Population: about 50. Hospitality: 100. This town is geared toward supporting cyclists.

By mid-afternoon it was hot and we pushed on toward Big Nelson Lake. I stopped to feed a donkey a bite of apple; he took it and ran off without so much as a thank you. The last fifteen miles were flat and scorching, past endless hayfields, fences, and glossy black cows. And grasshoppers. I really believed they would be edible, fried in some hot chili oil. I must be hungry.

When we reached Big Spencer Lake, we were stunned by its serenity. One couple who was already camped there in a camper, Kelly and Brian, welcomed us with sparkling water, beer, and chocolates. The lake was a perfect mirror, mountains reflected on its surface, broken only by the occasional fish jumping for a fly. It was the most peaceful place we'd seen. Tent sites tucked into the trees, a pebbled shoreline, pristine cool water for swimming. Our version of heaven. We were grateful we had chosen this place, a few miles off route.

We are keeping the rubber side down and making miles.

The Llama Farm (Really Alpacas…)

Day 14 - Tuesday, August 30
52 miles today • 483 miles total
To The Llama Farm (via Lincoln)

We crossed another peak of the Continental Divide today and arrived at the Llama Farm around 8 p.m., sleeping in a covered wagon that felt like a frontier Airbnb. The online reviews rave about this place, and they're right. It's called "The Llama Farm," but they're alpacas, adorable, judgy, and fluffy.

Barbara, the host, welcomes bikepackers free of charge and provides amenities that feel like treasure: a porch refrigerator filled with premade sandwiches, wine, drinks, jars of M&Ms, peanut butter, and just about anything a tired cyclist could want. Four or five funky little cabins dot the property. Barbara does not accept donations, she just asks that you pay it forward to someone down the line. We are happy to do that and generously tipped the waitress in the next café.

The morning ride to Lincoln was supposed to be easy, but I was tired and it felt anything but. We spent about three hours in town: bought a charging cord, ate huckleberry ice cream, and spent time at the library, inside and outside. My dad texted, "Where are you and what is that little building near you?" (Answer: At a picnic table in Lincoln, next to a library with Wi-Fi.)

My dad follows us on an app that tracks our location and progress. He also goes onto his virtual reality headset and walks through our destinations, sometimes providing valuable insight to us. Sometimes just asking questions out of curiosity. It is comforting to know he is watching out for us, even if it is from afar.

At the ice cream shop, I sat next to a man who looked like a worn-out rancher with a permanent scowl etched into his face. The kind of man you assume has never apologized for anything. He told me, without prompting, that he used to be a mean man. Then he had a stroke, and suddenly he needed help with everything. Being dependent humbled him, he said. Softened him. Made him better.

It was such a quiet, surprising moment of honesty, the kind that slips out only when someone has been stripped down to the studs and rebuilt by circumstance. He seemed at peace with his new reality. A forced change, but one he was grateful for. A better man. A better person. We need more of those in this world.

His honesty caught me off guard, not because men like him don't feel things, but because they rarely say them out loud. And it reminded me of a moment years earlier, when I was still wearing my own armor.

"We'd like to offer you the position of Technical Department Manager," Mark said.

"I want to be Plant Manager," I replied.

His eyes widened.

None of my former coworkers—all men, all older, all steeped in the paper-mill hierarchy—had ASKED for the top job. But I had decided my new job was better than going back to the paper mill in my old position. I would return only if I could turn it into a career move. I had the education, the experience, and apparently, the cajónes.

The transition from coworker to boss wasn't easy, but the moment that sealed it came during an interview for a store's manager. The interview panel consisted of one female department manager and five burly men from the mill—shaggy hair, beards, grease under their nails, and me, an intimidating "group" interview. The candidate, a man, looked around the table and asked, "So… who's the boss here?"

All five heads turned toward me.

"SHE is," one of them said.

The candidate blinked, stunned. His eyes darted from their faces to mine, trying to reconcile the thin woman in a button-down shirt with the idea of authority. "SHE is?" he said in disbelief.

I let the silence stretch just long enough, then said, "I have large ovaries."

The room erupted in laughter. The interview was effectively over. But the moment stuck with me—not because it was funny, but because it was the first time I said out loud what I'd been acting out for years: I wasn't waiting to be acknowledged. I was accepting that I had earned the position, even if I hadn't fully reconciled how.

And sitting there with my ice cream, I felt the echo of his story in my own. I hope I'm a better person now too, having stepped away from the competitive corporate world where "never enough" was the air we breathed. I'm learning to accept who I want to be. Who I was meant to be. Who I am.

An adventurer, not just in athletics, but in life. Camping in the backyard is an adventure. Riding into a new town is an adventure. Every day is an adventure, as I see the world.

By the time we rolled out of Lincoln, something in me had settled. The day hadn't gotten easier, but I had. Ice cream, humility, and a stranger's honesty will do that. We rode another four and a half hours, climbing a steep, loose-gravel rise where I had to push near the top. At the summit we met a couple of dirt-bike riders. From there, it was downhill to the farm, well worth the effort

We expected to reach Helena the next day.

COW POO PIES, CATTLE CROSSINGS, POO-PHORIA, POO-PHOBIA

Day 15 - Wednesday, August 31
40.7 miles today • 523.7 miles total
To Hot as Hell-ena and the BQuick Runner's Yard

We dubbed Helena "hot as Hell-ena," and we never want to go to Hell if it is this hot. The name fit.

The cows bellowed all night, clearly convinced the grass *just beyond* their fence was superior to the identical grass under their own hooves. Classic bovine FOMO (fear of missing out). As someone who has climbed a few metaphorical fences myself, I wanted to shout, "Just enjoy the clover on your side, cows!" Tara said they sounded like Chewbacca in the dark at 2 a.m.

Our covered-wagon accommodations were unexpectedly luxurious, complete with a giant jar of M&M's. The generosity of strangers continued to amaze me. If kindness were currency, Montana would be the Federal Reserve.

We rolled out around 9 a.m., which is late for a day forecasted to be hotter than Satan's armpit. Almost immediately we encountered a massive pile of bear scat, full of berry seeds. A real "Good morning, travelers!" from the local wildlife. Tara and I rode alone as Jon and Lois stayed back in Lincoln because Lois wasn't feeling well. Two more Continental Divide crossings brought our total to four, and we are now 522 miles into this 2,700-mile odyssey.

Somewhere along the winding roads, a realization hit us: when you spend hours staring at the road, braking downhill for eight or ten miles, scanning for potholes, gravel, and the occasional bear, you eventually learn that when cow poo becomes frequent, the cow itself is not far ahead. The poo-er replaces the poo pile. It's practically a law of nature and you need to look up.

We saw every variety of bovine beauty today: black cows, brown cows, white and brown cows, all lounging in the road like they owned the place. We executed several cow-avoidance maneuvers, which felt like slalom skiing but with more mooing. I love animals, often more than people, so I didn't mind the games.

I have not yet mentioned the cattle guards. These metal-bar death traps stretch across the road, between fence posts, spaced just wide enough to swallow a cow's hoof or a bike tire. The first time I crossed one I held my breath—gripped the handlebars in a death vise and tensed every muscle in my body—exactly the opposite of what you're supposed to do. After a few crossings, we learned to roll over them slowly, calmly, and with only mild terror. They've become so common now that we barely notice them… until one rattles your soul.

At one point I was certain I saw a grizzly, but we stopped well before reaching it. When we finally passed the spot, it had already vanished. Our streak of successful Grizzly Avoidance remained intact. Long may it continue.

At the top of our third pass, we met Kenny and Stephanie and immediately broke into a happy dance together. I loved their willingness to celebrate a tiny victory with full-body enthusiasm. Watching strangers embrace silliness helps me loosen my own emotional grip. Mimi would have adored the mountaintop dancing.

By the time we rolled into Helena, it was 95°F. The ride down into the town was like a blast furnace. We were out of water and feeling desperate. We stopped at the first building that appeared occupied. It was an auto repair shop, and they had a water cooler in the waiting room. Bliss. Salvation. Ask and ye shall receive.

One of Tara's panniers had broken, so we headed straight to the bike shop. We ended the day sleeping in BQuick Running's yard, locating it after some frustrating navigation. It was another unexpected but perfect accommodation.

Our Vocabulary of the Day was poo-centered. Perhaps our brains were cooked, as we devolved into silly adolescent humor. I attributed these to Tara's nursing experience but wholeheartedly agreed with them.

Poo-phoria

That glorious moment *before* you get on the bike when you know, deep in your soul and your colon, that you're done for the day. You feel light. Cleansed. Practically aerodynamic.

Poo-phobia

The opposite. The creeping dread after a questionable burger when you fear you'll be stopping every twenty minutes, praying to the roadside gods, and possibly never reaching your destination.

There's always a day on a long trip when the bottom drops out, when fatigue stops being a feeling and becomes a worldview. Mine arrived with the heat in Hell-ena. I wasn't crying, but perhaps only because the heat had sucked every drop of fluid from me. The lack of hydration coupled with the lack of energy required for crying. The Divide has a way of stripping you down to whatever truth is underneath, and on that day, the truth was simple: I was hot, tired, and worried the heat was going to permanently affect our bodies.

In that hollowed-out space, my mind went to the moment everything changed for Leigh, not because my struggle matched hers, but because endurance has a way of pulling old memories to the surface, especially the ones that taught you what real grit looks like.

I flew into Geneva, Illinois, just west of Chicago, to provide moral support for Leigh and Brad during her recovery. I watched her limp around the railing Brad had built in the center of their driveway, a six-foot loop of two-by-fours that became her training ground. She steadied herself with her left hand as she lifted her right foot with a hitch, using momentum to clear the ground. Without that hitch, her foot dragged. To a stranger, she might have looked like she'd had a stroke, her entire right side weakened.

One step at a time, she moved counterclockwise, her right arm hanging uselessly at her side. At the end of the railing, she turned left, took three careful steps, and started up the other side. Hitch, swing, drag. Again. And again. Her foot drooped more as she tired, but she kept going, wearing a faint path into the tarmac. She wasn't breathing hard, but the concentration was draining her. Still, she finished her five laps, the goal she'd set for herself, just two weeks after brain surgery for a cancerous tumor.

The girl who once ran beside me through Barcelona, laughing at the Nose Man and choking down sour grapes, was now fighting for every inch of movement. And I stood there, watching her circle that wooden railing, feeling the weight of how much had changed, and how much strength she still carried.

It's hard to believe that just six weeks earlier, a small group of family and friends had gathered in Zion National Park for Leigh and Brad's wedding. At twenty-five and thirty-two, they were young, adventurous, ambitious, reshuffling their spring wedding to the fall because of COVID travel restrictions, but unfazed by the disruption. They were glowing, full of plans, standing in one of the most beautiful places on earth.

And then, after returning home, everything changed.

A devastating seizure.

An ambulance ride.

A night in the emergency room.

A week later, brain surgery.

How can someone move away from family for a spouse and career and end up living within reach of one of the best brain surgeons in the country? Coincidence or providence, I still don't know.

I was in Florida for a business conference the night of the seizure. My sister Angela, Leigh's mom, called in the middle of the night, but I didn't hear it. I went out for a run early the next morning, still oblivious. When I finally checked my phone and returned her call, the news hollowed me out. I couldn't imagine being her mother. I couldn't imagine being her husband. I was devastated, as her aunt.

Leigh had been evaluating ways to pursue her dreams, considering a career change and more education. She was encouraging me to pursue my dreams. I was envious of her self-awareness and her willingness to pursue something more than a job. At her age, I didn't have the self-knowledge or the courage to seek out my passions, let alone follow them. I stayed on the career treadmill, afraid to make a change I might regret. I told myself my jobs enabled my lifestyle of chasing vacation adventures. Later in life, I tried not to dwell on the choices I didn't make sooner.

Now for Leigh, the long stretch of treatment: surgery, chemotherapy, radiation, and month after month of brain-imaging, hoping and praying for no recurrence. Every time I received a text with her scan results, my heart jumped to my throat until I read the words: still clean. Eventually the scans moved to every three months. They will continue indefinitely.

Out on the Divide, grinding up that endless climb through the heat into Hell, I felt the echo of those years, the fear, the vigilance, the stubborn hope. My legs were tired, but they worked. My lungs burned, but they filled. And the trail, indifferent as ever, kept rising. I kept rising with it.

Powered by Pastries
High on the Lows and Low on the Highs

Day 16 - Thursday, September 1
50.47 miles today • 574.17 total
To Merry Widow Health Mine Campground

I love the start of a new month. Rabbit, rabbit. A superstition that promises good luck if you say it first thing on the first day. I'm superstitious enough to say it, yet stubborn enough to believe you make your own luck. Apparently, I'm capable of holding contradictory beliefs with complete conviction. Useful on a trip like this, like believing the man was perfectly sane, but leaving the scene as if he was anything but, perhaps even a serial killer.

We needed all the luck we could get.

From the BQuick Runner's yard, the sun had set and then rose, on both trajectories, as a brilliant red orb, beautiful, ominous, and confusing. Red sky at night, sailors' delight. Red sky in morning, sailors' warning. Hard to know which one applied when you're up before dawn, packing your tent in the dark in a city yard and rolling out by 7 a.m., red sky aglow.

We stopped at Park Avenue Coffee for pastries. We were always thinking of Mimi when it came to pastries! Then we headed up Grizzly Gulch. We chose the alternate route: seven miles longer but supposedly less climbing. Supposedly. We still climbed over 4,000 feet, partly because our navigation system, Ben (Bike Navigator) had a meltdown. Ben is trustworthy only when he's following the magenta line, named Maggie. When Ben is with Maggie, all is well. Today he was supposed to follow the blue line, and that was apparently beyond his pay grade and separated him from Maggie, not allowable.

We got turned around twice. The first time, a pair of farmers herding cows with a pickup and a four-wheeler gave us directions, after asking if we wanted to buy a cow. I needed the laugh; I was already hot, tired, and flirting with demoralization.

The second wrong turn led to a very... memorable encounter. We were standing under an overpass in the shade, having ridden up a steep grade, while questioning the route accuracy. We were trying to decipher the map when an older man drove up. He seemed overly eager to help, and the hair on the back of my neck stood up. He told us he was the only one who lived on that road, had two ponds and two dogs, and we were welcome to camp in his yard. Kind? Creepy? Serial abductor? Hard to say. My gut whispered caution; my brain told my gut to stop being dramatic. Classic me. Still trying to learn to take my gut seriously.

If it had been two hours later, we might have taken him up on the offer. Would we have found serenity by a pond with mountain views? He offered to have a friend vouch for him. Or would we have become a Dateline-episode? I'd love to interview his nonexistent neighbors.

We were still in Montana, after all, home of the Unabomber. (For the record, he was from Illinois but lived in a cabin in Montana.) Comforting.

He offered us water. My instinct is always to decline help, but I'm trying to learn that accepting kindness is not weakness. I took the water and was grateful.

He helped us with the map, then abruptly asked if we were lesbians. It was jarring, and again my instincts prickled. We told him we'd been married, collectively, for fifty-six years to our male husbands. He then assured us the nearby town of Basin was very lesbian friendly. Hmmm. As we rode away, Tara said we should've asked him if he was a serial killer, just to clear the air.

We rolled back down the hill and found the correct route, not following Ben or Maggie. We passed through Clancy and Jefferson City, which barely qualified as towns. Steady Freddy (Tara) pulled us along while Spaghetti (me) struggled up yet another hill. Every morning, I ask, "You ready, Freddy?" and Tara replies, "I'm ready, Spaghetti." Today, Spaghetti was al dente at best.

At the top of the mother fucker of a hill, I was overheated, exhausted, and very crabby. But after flying down the other side and cooling off in the breeze, my mood lifted. Amazing what a descent—and surviving a possible serial killer encounter—can do for morale.

We battled our first steady, quartering wind of the trip. After a gas-station feast of chips, Gatorade, a Klondike bar, a Slurpee, and sparkling water, we finished the day strong, considering my near-meltdown. I think I whined most of the way, but I pedaled every mile to our stop at the mine campground.

The signs around the Merry Widow Mine claim that radon is healthy for you. What?! Should we visit the radon mine for its "therapeutic effects"? Absolutely not. Back home we install radon-remediation systems in our basements. Here, someone preys on desperately sick people by offering radon-therapy. What killed the Merry Widow's husband? I have my suspicions.

Late in the day, when strange encounters resurface in your mind, I found myself thinking about the man under the overpass. In the moment he'd set off every internal alarm I had, but as the miles passed, I wondered if he was simply lonely. Awkward. Human in that slightly off-kilter way people can be when they don't get much practice at connection.

It reminded me of an employee I once had who showed up to my manufacturing plant wearing only one shoe because he didn't want to be late. He'd sprinted out the door, having run out of time to find the match and arrive at work on time, so he left home, committed to the probationary attendance policy. Earnest. Irrational. Trying his best, even if he was shoeless.

There's something comforting about that kind of imperfect effort, the reminder that most people aren't malicious or dangerous. They're just navigating their own private storms, their own missing-shoe mornings, their own awkward attempts at being helpful. We all have our challenges. Some of us just wear them more visibly.

The map error made less sense or maybe I cared less about making sense of it. I've spent most of my life trying to control outcomes, people, plans. But the trail keeps reminding me the best moments happen when you stop gripping the handlebars so tightly.

Mines and No Minds

Day 17 - Friday, September 2
37.2 miles today • 611.37 total
To Butte, Montana

The morning started chilly, which felt like a blessing after yesterday's heat had wrung me out like a damp dishrag. We were up early and rolling by 8 a.m., enjoying the cool air while it lasted.

The campground was filled with people who appeared to be there for "therapy sessions" in the radon mine, bonnets, long skirts, and a general reluctance to return a friendly hello. It felt like we had stumbled into a quiet, bonneted subculture of radioactive wellness.

We rode uphill until 11:30 a.m. Yes, half of today's mileage was Up, capital U. The theme of the day was mines. We passed two on the route, and Butte itself boasts one of the largest open-pit mines in the world. More than a mile wide, visible from anywhere in town, and impossible to ignore. Our first glimpse of it came as we descended toward the city, a massive scar in the earth that somehow still managed to be impressive.

We reached Butte early in the afternoon after duly following Maggie's magenta navigation line. We checked into the city KOA campground. The best part was a cold swimming pool. After days of heat, it felt like baptism.

Lunch was by a stone cabin we passed on the way in, and during the final climb a giant caterpillar inched across the road, moving about as fast as I felt. My legs were spent, sluggish, and protesting every pedal stroke.

Dinner was sushi, which felt wildly out of place in a mining town but tasted excellent. I inhaled fried rice with what could only be described as a bucket of soy sauce, the salt desperately needed.

By 8 p.m., we still hadn't set up our tents because it was too hot, even with the sun sinking. At least we managed showers and laundry, which significantly improved our odor profile. We hoped to be able to sleep in the noisy campground tucked beside the freeway.

> In my first year of retirement, a full year before the Divide, I signed up for my first ultramarathon, a backyard ultra at Pineland Farms. A 4.2-mile loop every hour, starting on the hour. I was fifty-six, newly retired, wary of aging, and trying to outrun the freight train of diminishing physical ability I saw in friends and family. I didn't want to wait until my body said no. I wanted to try while it still said maybe.
>
> Training was hot, muggy, messy, full of deer, mushrooms, wet feet, fog, and the quiet fear that I might be dreaming too big. The week before the race I even fell carrying a kayak, slipping on algae in Crocs. Part of me wondered if I'd subconsciously tried to sabotage myself. But I showed up anyway, because sometimes showing up is the most difficult part of the battle.
>
> I ran lap after lap, with friends, alone, in the dark, through fields that felt endless. My quads screamed, my

> calves "joined the party," and by the tenth lap my shoulders were hunched around my ears like a turtle retreating into its shell. My body finally said, *enough.* My support crew, a.k.a. my sister Angela asked, "do you want me to push you to go on?" My body said "no." And for once, I listened. I stopped at forty-two miles, my stretch goal, and felt something I hadn't expected: satisfaction. Pride. A quiet, fierce joy. A feeling of accomplishment.
>
> Driving home, nauseated and exhausted, I realized something important: I could do hard things. Long things. Scary things. Things that required stubbornness and grit and a willingness to suffer. Completing the Divide would demand all of that. But the ultramarathon had already shown me who I was becoming, someone who didn't quit, someone who could stay steady for hours, someone who could trust her body to carry her farther than her mind believed. Someone not afraid to live her dreams.

And maybe that's why this day felt so grounded. It's still early in this adventure, but somewhere inside me was the memory of that long day at Pineland, the proof that I can keep moving, keep showing up, keep finding the next mile. Confidence doesn't arrive all at once; it accumulates quietly, like miles on a bike or loops on a trail.

Tyson Gives Us Lettuce

Day 18 - Saturday, September 3
39.2 miles today • 650 total
To Beaver Dam Campground

We continue to meet amazing and generous people on our bikes. Last night, at a steak and sushi restaurant, the waitress let us bring our bicycles inside. We'd ridden a bike path from the KOA into the town of Butte and were worried about leaving the bikes outside, so her kindness felt like one of those small trail graces you don't forget.

Back at the campground, Tyson, camped near us in a purple Jeep, gave us a head of lettuce grown vertically and hydroponically by his neighbor in Calgary. Tyson was traveling with his dog, Po, on his way to pick up his wife in Phoenix. They were spending a month exploring back-roads and off-road jeep trails. We got a later start this morning because we enjoyed chatting with him. I was anxious to get riding, though. I struggle with idle chitchat when I know a hot, difficult day is ahead. I love people, but when I have a mission, my social patience evaporates.

We rode a bike path for two miles to rejoin the route, then stopped at Ace Hardware for stove fuel. From there, we climbed through the single-track in Thompson Park, stopping at the bottom of the ascent to soak our arm warmers and kerchiefs in a cold stream. One section was so steep I had to remove my panniers, push the bike up, then walk back down to retrieve the bags. A glamorous sport, bikepacking.

We met a woman on the trail who owned a bike shop in Butte. She told us to reach out if we needed anything, another example of the trail's quiet generosity. The single-track was fantastic, and it felt good to be on a real trail again.

Near the top of the climb, we ran into four Spaniards. Their English was limited and our Spanish non-existent. Their first question was, "Do you have husbands?" My immediate thought: *Why would you ask that?* Followed quickly by: *Should we be concerned?* We shared snacks and laughter, and despite the heat, they seemed like a cheerful, gregarious group.

The descent through sagebrush was spectacular. The Spaniards flew downhill like they had rockets strapped to their bikes. I loved the breeze and the steepness, just enough to require focus so I didn't launch myself into the brush. But at the bottom, the heat hit us like we'd opened the door to a preheated oven. Breathing felt heavy and suffocating, as if the air pressed against my lungs instead of filling them.

We found a green, slime-filled cow creek, repulsive but gloriously cold. We soaked our sleeves, shirts, and neckerchiefs, then put them back on sopping wet before the final climb to Beaver Dam. The landscape had shifted again, now dotted with large rock piles. My legs were tired, my mind was tired, and the heat was relentless. It was a mentally brutal day.

But the campsite was lovely, and nothing tastes better than instant potatoes and tuna after a long, hot ride, especially when you've had fresh lettuce for lunch.

Some Divide days blur together, climb up, then down, up, then down, miles that feel identical, scenery that shifts only in subtle ways. The same rhythm of pedal, shift, coast, repeat. It isn't suffering, exactly. It's more like being absorbed into the machinery of the day, carried forward by momentum rather than motivation.

> Months later, after the ride was behind me, I kept thinking about Leigh walking that loop in their driveway. Not the hitch or the drag—I'd already memorized those—but the rhythm of it. The steadiness. The way she circled that six-foot track with no promise of glory, no finish-line music, just the quiet insistence of someone determined to reclaim her life inch by inch.
>
> Her long stretch after surgery had its own cadence: the slow rebuilding, the therapies, the scans that never really end. Nothing about it was optional or chosen. Nothing about it was recreational. But there was a persistence in her, a kind of strength that doesn't announce itself—it simply keeps going. There was nothing cinematic about that period. No triumphant soundtrack, just the slow, grinding work of healing and waiting, healing and waiting.
>
> Looking back, I can see how those quiet Divide days gave me a language—not for what Leigh endured, but for the steadiness it required. A recognition, not a comparison. A way of understanding persistence in its smallest, most unremarkable form. My own miles weren't heroic. They were simply steady. And sometimes steady is enough.

Expansive Views in British Columbia. Photo: T. Kaplan

Tara and Mimi headed to the Airbnb. Photo: J. Cusick

Dusty Riding in the Peter Lougheed Provincial Park, Canada. Photo: J. Cusick

Stealth Camping. Colorado. Photo: T. Kaplan

Thin and hungry. Photos: T. Kaplan

Marshall Pass. Photo Credit: T. Kaplan

Chaco Trading Post. Jon on the railcar. Photo: T. Kaplan

Inside Camping. Nightly Planning Session. Photo: J. Cusick

Gatorade or Guilty? Photo: J. Cusick

Aspen Alley. Photo: J. Cusick

Foreboding weather. Photo: J. Cusick

Headed to Pie Town. Photo: T. Kaplan

TLC Ranch. Photo: J. Cusick

The Finish. Photo: L. Kaplan

The Finish. Photo: T. Kaplan

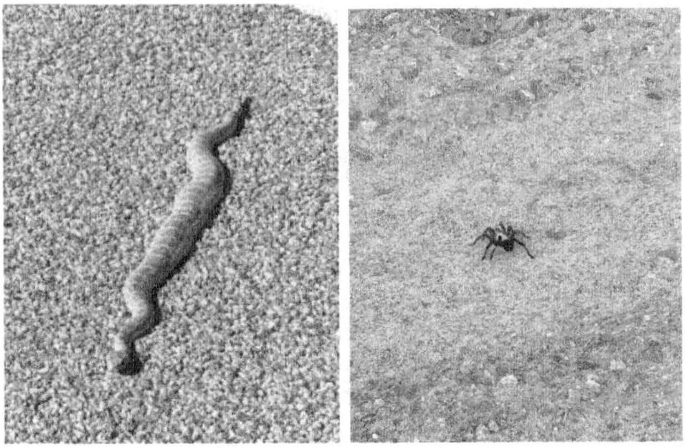

Rattler and Tarantula. Photo: J. Cusick

Packing for Home. Photo: J. Cusick

Chapter 6: The Mirror the Trail Holds Up

One Year Performance Review

Before the bike trip, one year into my "retirement" as an under-employed lazy American, I decided it was time for a performance review. A self-evaluation, if you will. Me! Me! Me! My life had become gloriously self-centered, a full-time job really, and I needed to know: how many retirement goals had I crushed? How many had I failed? And how many could I still check off before leaving for the Great Divide?

With six months to go before the bike trip, I took a 30,000-foot view of my life. (This was the only altitude at which my decisions made sense.)

The Bureau of Labor Statistics reported that 4.4 million people voluntarily quit their jobs in February 2022. A Flex Jobs survey said 62% left due to toxic culture. Other articles said Americans were just lazy. I left because of Door #1, but I was fully embracing Door #2. If laziness was the diagnosis, I was finally living my truth.

I left because my wage no longer compensated for the circus management had become. The company had gone from valuing long-term commitment and FDA-level rigor to churning through employees like a woodchipper set to "fine." Enough about that.

I still flirted with the idea of a second career. I had tried for years to break into environmental work, but apparently decades in corporate America gave off a faint odor of "might ask for a salary." Hard to say whether my CV whispered "indolent."

Our financial plan supported not returning to the "real" workforce, and for now I was living life on my own terms—not horizontal, and not welded to a desk chair.

I had no regrets. I was one of those post-pandemic, sort-of non-working Americans who were supposedly too young to retire but too old to tolerate nonsense. One of those indifferent Americans blamed for poor customer service, supply-chain issues, and probably the decline of Western civilization. Yet despite the criticism, I was far too tired to consider working. Where had all the workers gone? I didn't know, but I hoped they were someplace with better snacks.

I did work a few hours a week for a group protecting local drinking water. The job ad had said "part-time, intermittent, and temporary," which was exactly the level of commitment I was willing to give anything that wasn't a bike ride or a nap. The pay was a fraction of my former wage, with no benefits, and I covered taxes and travel expenses. A dream job, really, if your dream was to slowly go broke while saving the environment.

As a non-worker, I was also actively depleting 40 years of frugal savings. Neither of us had a serious pension. If Social Security collapsed before we could collect, we might be in trouble, but would we even live long enough? Several friends hadn't. At the time of retirement, the stock market had immediately erased 2.5 years of planned income from my 401K. Again, oh well. What was money for, if not to spend before a long-term care facility billed you $14,000 a month to keep you alive against your will?

With no children to support, I had shifted from frugally saving to living my dreams. It was both terrifying and exhilarating. John continued to work and happily stayed home to care for the cat. If he had a pile of dirt and a tractor, he was content. I admired a man with simple needs.

So, what had I accomplished this past year as a lazy, under-employed individual?

- I visited retired friends in Florida, where they taught me essential retirement skills like relaxing and drinking PBR hard coffee for breakfast. Exhausting.
- I "helped" a friend scout a Grand Canyon trip. I was far too lazy for this life.
- I spent more time with family. My nine-year-old niece said, "Aunt Jenny, I've seen you more this year than in all my previous eight years." Nothing like a child to deliver a performance review.
- Weekly card games with my mom and sisters. This was the most stressful part of my week. The competitiveness remained; the fun vices were gone.

- I went to Hudson Bay and saw polar bears in the wild. They were working harder than I was.
- I volunteered on a tour in Iceland. It was work, but unpaid, so I could muster the ambition.
- I ran the Millinocket Half-Marathon, where the water stops were full-on bars. My early spring "training" with PBR hard coffee had prepared me well.
- I launched a dream business: RunBoothbayMaine. One runner signed up, then canceled. I refunded him. End of that effort. In my old life, I'd have called it a failure. In retirement, it was a success: I mapped routes, marketed, set prices, and shared my love of running as I ran the planned routes with family and friends. That was enough. Also, I was too lazy to want to run with anyone.
- I became a licensed Maine Sea Kayaking Guide. I aspired to guide tourists along the coast, though I warned them that Maine had only three seasons: almost winter, winter, and still winter.
- I joined the YMCA and met dear friends.
- I occasionally worried about my low white blood cell count and the benzene I had washed my hands in during my paper mill days. But worrying burned calories, so I tried not to overdo it.

My biggest personal triumph that year was the achievement of the lifelong dream of running the ultramarathon. Months of training, and I had done it. I was lazy, but apparently not that lazy. Proof that normal people can achieve big things.

Now, with six months before the big bike ride, I was deciding what to train for. Should I run a few miles, so the May marathon doesn't destroy me? Should I hike with cans of beans in my backpack to prepare for hiking the GR5 in the French Alps? Or should I ride my bike, since the Continental Divide might be my demise? Or maybe a nap, and work on the resting-preparation phase.

I was already looking forward to returning home after the GDMBR trip. After the ride, I will have earned the right to be lazy.

Fleecer Ridge and Smoky Vistas

Day 19 — Sunday, September 4
37.4 miles today • 687.97 miles total
To Little Joe

We left Beaver Dam in the cold, about 35°F. Within twenty-five minutes we were peeling off hats, tights, jackets, and mittens as we climbed the storied Fleecer Ridge. The cows were frequent impediments to any morning speed. There were plenty of them, many standing squarely in the road, and some were clearly bulls, so we passed with caution. We kept checking their nether regions, assuming testicles equaled danger. All encounters were peaceful. The calves were the wariest, staring at us until fear overtook them and they skittered into the sagebrush.

Early in the climb I heard a "ting, ting, ting" behind me. Tara was leaking quarters onto the road. We checked her pockets and panniers, no holes. We started again. "Ting, ting." More quarters. We never did figure out where they were escaping from, but we're now committed to spending them to reduce weight.

We climbed over the infamous Fleecer Ridge, known for being so steep it's considered unrideable. Tara rode the whole thing UP; I only pushed a bit. We overshot the turn, of course, and climbed farther than necessary. Ugh. The descent is even more infamous in our north-to-south direction: a quarter mile so steep we had to walk in the sagebrush, holding our steeds back and holding our breath to avoid tumbling or sliding. The rocks were loose, the footing slippery, and there was no way to ride it with bikes as heavy as ours or tires as thin as ours. This section makes a strong argument for mountain bikes and fat tires.

Smoke from distant forest fires hung in the air, muting the views. After making it down safely, we collapsed into the shade for a break. Our next stop was the one-horse town of Wise River, where we picked up supplies—which, for us, almost always meant food. It was hot. So hot. Breathing felt like inhaling from a furnace. Every day we were amazed by the temperature swing, convinced each morning that it couldn't possibly get as hot as the day before, and every afternoon proven wrong. The mountains around us looked as if they were actively eroding, piles of loose rubble slumped at their feet.

We reached Little Joe campsite, bathed in the river, and met a wonderful group of campers in their sixties who offered us food. We accepted an avocado and a fresh lime for our bean tortillas, plus melon and salty pistachios. Later we joined them for birthday wine and brownies. Trail magic at its finest.

Laurie Is Amazingly Kind and Generous

Day 20 — Monday, September 5
16.4 miles today • 704.37 miles total
To Laurie and Gregg's

We left Little Joe after 9:30 a.m. Before rolling out, a German couple, Regina and her husband, pedaled past, spotted us, and stopped to chat. There's an instant connection with other bikepackers. More of our kind of people, as shared suffering is bonding. Tara is quick to exchange contact information; I'm more hesitant, especially when tired. My mind closes in on itself, especially later in the day, and talking to strangers takes energy I don't always have.

Tara has been struggling to keep track of her tent stakes. We swear they play hide-and-seek in the grass, hoping to be left behind. Her supply had dwindled to the point of crisis. As fate would have it, Regina sold her a few extras. They attempted a hat barter, but Regina wouldn't part with her beloved hat in exchange for one of Tara's favorites, a rainbow design.

Then, as if the morning needed more delight, Jon and Lois appeared. We didn't expect to see them until tomorrow, so their arrival felt like another trail gift. I found that traveling with others eased the pressure I put on myself. New conversations, shared pacing, and the comfort of familiar faces all softened the edges of the day. Definitely "our people".

Tara had arranged for us to visit her friends Laurie and Greg, whom she met in India. On the way, we stopped at a crystal mine and dug up a few treasures, more weight for the packs. Noooo. Jon, Tara, and I dug in the dirt while Lois lounged across a picnic table, soaking up the sun. Her fatigue had a cause she would discover months later.

When we arrived at Laurie and Greg's home, Laurie fed us immediately, and we fell in love on the spot. Sausages on the grill, pasta salad, potatoes, veggie salad, pure heaven. After showers and phone calls, Laurie drove us to Dillon for shopping. Few purchases were made as they all add weight, but we polished off a box of gluten-free Oreos on the drive home. Then Laurie made dinner: corn, elk steaks, halibut, and baked beans made with both bacon and venison. Sleeping in a bed felt luxurious.

We LOVE, LOVE, LOVE Laurie.

We Love the People Who Host and Feed Us

Day 21 - Tuesday, September 6
44 miles today • 748.37 total
To Hansen Ranch

We had a big breakfast with Laurie and Greg and leaving them felt like trying to pry ourselves away from gravity. Greg, an emergency room physician, had worked the evening shift the night before, so we hadn't seen him until morning. He greeted us with burritos made from venison sausage, endless coffee, fruit, OJ, toast with butter and homemade jam. We LOVE Greg. We LOVE Laurie. We did not want to leave. Their generosity was very much appreciated.

As an ER physician, Greg talked with Tara and me about Mimi's accident. His calm, thoughtful assessment reassured us that we had done everything right. He believed the sternum rub and our efforts to bring Mimi back to consciousness may have saved her life. I floated my non-medical theory that perhaps letting the brain "rest" while unconscious might help it heal. He did not subscribe to this idea. Consciousness, he reminded us, is better than the alternative; the body works more effectively when the brain is engaged.

After breakfast, Greg reviewed our first-aid kits. I welcomed the chance to ditch any weight. We removed some miscellaneous detritus and added meat tenderizer for bee stings, Greg's recommendation. Of all things. He didn't specify which ingredient worked the magic, but we trusted him.

It was after 11 a.m. when we finally left, grateful for the food, the rest, and the slower start. On our way out of town, we stopped at the post office to pick up a map Larry had mailed and to send home a package of "excess stuff." A shirt, a battery, a spare bike light, and a few items I had not yet used and therefore deemed unnecessary, and which had been gaining weight in my psyche for days. I was relieved the postal clerk didn't ask about batteries; I would not have been able to lie, and I would still be carrying that weight. Guilty of lying by omission? She didn't ask. The relief of the reduced weight counterbalanced the guilt.

The tiny post office had an outhouse attached directly to the building. Not a flush toilet. A real outhouse. With a very large spider. It made for a quick morning elimination.

We set off on a twenty-mile flat stretch toward Bannack State Park. Tara became the engine, pulling three train cars behind her, and we made record time. She has certainly earned the "diesel" moniker. We ate lunch at a picnic table, extra burritos and fruit Laurie had packed for us, plus fruit tea, the never-ending generosity of the most appreciated kind. The landscape had shifted to sagebrush and prairie grasses, the air dry and the wind relentless.

Mid-afternoon, Laurie drove out and met us on the road, to hand-deliver our map, which had arrived after we left the post office. Her kindness was endless.

Our next stop was a bar in Grant. We ordered four ice creams with caramel sauce, three sodas, and a beer. The bar also sold enormous cinnamon buns and massive rice-crispy squares. Mimi would have loved the cinnamon bun; it was the size of a dinner plate. I bought a five-inch tall rice-crispy square, ate half immediately, and saved the rest for later.

The people were friendly, the service good, and the calories appreciated, but the proprietor warned us that the septic system odor made camping unpleasant. We rode on.

The wind felt like a furnace, dry lips, dry skin, wetted sleeves drying in minutes. Seven more miles brought us to Hansen Ranch, a fantastic choice.

And somewhere in those hot, wind-blasted miles, my mind drifted to a very different kind of heat, the kind that comes from responsibility pressing down on you from all sides.

> The night before payroll, I had called the bank to confirm the deposit had arrived. It hadn't. The bank manager encouraged me to call again in the morning. I did. Still nothing.
>
> "Where is the money from our paper sales being deposited?" I asked Nancy, the controller I had hired, the brilliant, uncredentialed woman I trusted more than any of the arrogant, educated men we'd interviewed. "If we wait a bit longer and call the bank again, perhaps the deposit will have been made," I said. She replied, "it's your dream, make it as big as you want." She is honest, forthright and frank, all the reasons I love her. I kept dreaming but it was not to be.
>
> We laughed but then she said, "Not into our accounts in Vermont."
>
> The mill's new owner, rumored to be shipping arms to Iran, had been siphoning revenue elsewhere. And now I had over a hundred employees who wouldn't be paid. Again.
>
> I stood in front of them in the break room and said the words no leader wants to say: "We can't make payroll. When the funds arrive, I'll call you back in, if we can get enough raw material to start the paper machine." Eventually the owner went to federal prison. Thankfully, I bailed out prior to that event.
>
> They stayed. They supported me. Desperate people do desperate things, and rural New Englanders are nothing if not loyal. We limped along for months, shutting down when we ran

out of pulp or fuel, starting up again when just enough money trickled in to buy more.

I should have listened to my instincts sooner. But I stayed because they stayed. Because leadership, at its core, is a kind of love, even when it breaks your heart.

And as the wind pushed against us that afternoon, I felt the echo of that old weight, the familiar strain of holding things together when the foundation is crumbling. The trail has a way of quieting the noise, leaving only the truths you've carried for years.

Some loads were never mine to carry.

Some loads I carried anyway.

And some loads, like today's miles, I carry because they lead me somewhere better.

A sign welcomed bikers to camp on the ranch lands. No people, just a big yellow dog and a spectacular sunset. It was a sprawling ranch, oddly quiet, without another soul around. We made dinner sitting on a hay-wagon trailer. The shower, complete with fresh towels, earned a "9" on our bathroom scale. It would have been a "10" if it had included a glass of wine.

Not in Our Tents Tonight

Day 22—Wednesday, September 7
53 miles today • 801.37 total
Hansen Ranch to Dell

Today was our longest mileage day yet. Fifty-three miles. We are getting stronger. Twenty-five miles and five hours to reach the high point of the day, then a long descent through the spectacular Sheep Creek Valley. Tall rock walls, erosion-carved nooks and crannies, caves tucked into the cliffs. Three fishermen pointed out a mother black bear with two cubs heading up the valley.

The last three or four miles were tough, we were tired, but the terrain was essentially flat.

The road stretched out in a long, indifferent line, and my mind did what it always does when given too much space: it went back. I thought about the paper mill closing, the job I would have stayed in forever if the universe hadn't padlocked the doors. That was the first time I learned reinvention isn't always a bold choice; sometimes it's what you do when the floor disappears. One of the best compliments I received after these years, from a former coworker whom I greatly respected, "You have an amazing ability to reinvent yourself." He meant it sincerely, unlike others who assessed my many job changes in a less complimentary light.

My path would have been like my dad, a long-term employee, but instead my trajectory became that of a millennial. Nine jobs, nine changes and a lot of reinventions. An MBA, pursuit of a master's degree in environmental science, that I would not finish, just eleven credits shy of completion. In retrospect, the variety and learning kept me challenged. Kept me interested. The moves strengthening our marriage. I hope I contributed to the personal growth of some of the employees over the years as some did for me. Clement, a young Human Resources Manager at one facility I managed, knew I pined for an adventurous, outdoor life, and always encouraged me to go for my dreams. Well, Clem, it took a few years, but I am truly living my dreams now. Today, my business card says "Adventurer."

Before reaching our planned waypoint, we stopped at the Dell gas station for food. When we continued to the designated camping spot indicated on our map, we discovered it was no longer an option. The house was abandoned, the lawn a sparse hayfield, the whole area forlorn and rundown. Debris was scattered among clumps of tall, dry grass. It looked like no one had lived there in years. Sometimes our apps and the internet fail us. It was a "no-go," not even rating on our campground scale.

We backtracked to the gas station, passing three or four newly built log cabins. Could we get into one of those? Inside the store, we wandered the aisles in a daze, post long-day brain fog making even gas-station food decisions difficult. The cashier told us we could rent one of the cabins.

We stepped outside to weigh our options. Eight more miles to the next campsite after our longest day yet, or a cabin? Before we could decide, the wind snapped to life, sending sand and dust spiraling around us. A few cold raindrops hit our arms. Smoke from the fire to the west thickened, and a wall of dark clouds gathered in the distance. It felt less like coincidence and more like a warning.

Decision made.

We booked the cabin, bought beans, eggs, and toast for dinner, a British staple according to Jon and Lois, and settled into a cozy evening in a cozy cabin.

Blixen Flies!

Day 23 - Thursday, September 8
66 miles today • 867.37 miles total
To Red Rocks National Wildlife Refuge

Blixen, my reindeer ride, flew sixty-six miles today. He is gender-fluid, a combination of Santa's Blitzen and a vixen, with the preferred pronouns he/him/his. No disrespect intended. Had gender fluidity been acceptable when I was in seventh grade, when I scored high in spatial orientation on a career placement exam that recommended auto mechanic, only to be told girls weren't auto mechanics, I would definitely have chosen gender fluidity. But I digress.

The four of us and our rides cranked out sixty-six miles with a couple of variables in our favor:

- sometimes we were running downwind,
- sometimes it blew on our port beam,

all of which were better than off the bow, a.k.a. "head- on". The heat finally broke; it was in the 70s. Still smoky, but manageable. Only 2,400 feet of elevation gain and no long climbs. We left the cabin early, no tents to pack, and ate leftover beans and eggs for breakfast.

Nine miles brought us to Lima (as in Lima bean), population 221. The hardware store had dehydrated meals and epoxy for a temporary repair to Tara's wheel. One spoke had cracked the rim, adding a new anxiety. She'll get a new wheel in Pinedale, having called ahead to make plans with the bike shop, still five days away. Here's hoping it holds. Jon needed a new wheel in Helena, and Kenny, another rider, is also waiting for one to arrive. The pounding and washboard vibrations take their toll.

The bikes are miraculous, as are our bodies, to endure the daily beating. A night of sleep provides magical recovery.

We stocked up at the gas station for two days of food and enjoyed the riding—expansive rangeland, mountains, endless fencing. We stopped for snacks and lunch, then visited the ranger at the Red Rocks National Wildlife Refuge headquarters for a fire update. A small fire smoldered near tomorrow's route, but the roads remained open.

We hoped to see trumpeter swans as we camped at the refuge. The sunset was a spectacular red fireball through the smoke. We bathed in a cold stream feeding the lake. The four Spaniards we'd seen days earlier were here too, tired, quiet and resting. Bow hunters are camped nearby, preparing for elk season. Zzzzz.

Corn Dogs Save the Day

Day 24 - Friday, September 9
36.6 miles today • 904.27 miles total
To Big Springs

We entered Idaho, state number two, and I had a corn dog for the first time in my life. A corn dog, for the uninitiated (which apparently was just me), is a sausage or hot dog on a stick, dipped in cornmeal batter and deep-fried. Salty, fatty, corny perfection. I'd never been so desperate for calories, and never had a food so questionable in origin tasted so divine. A lot happened that day—cold temperatures, a reroute because of the Sawtell Peak forest fire, another Continental Divide crossing—but the corn dog looms largest in my memory. If not for the reroute, I would have missed it entirely. You never forget your first time. Hmmm, I am not going to go there.

We began the day packing up at Upper Red Rock Lake in the National Wildlife Refuge. The lake is expansive but shallow, and there were more ducks on the water than I've ever seen. No trumpeter swans, though I had hoped for them. The morning felt like our coldest yet. Within minutes of riding, we stopped to add more layers, neck warmers pulled over our noses, doubled mittens, jackets zipped so high the zippers nipped our skin. It was around 30°F when we woke, and although the air was still, the wind created by riding felt wintry. We envied the hunters' canvas tent with its woodstove puffing smoke into the sky. They were far warmer than we were.

We crossed the Continental Divide at Red Rock Pass and performed our divide-crossing happy-dance with Jon and Lois and a couple of mooing cows. Just after Henry's Lake, we stopped at a store in an RV park to warm up with cocoa and to find a neck warmer for Tara. She'd been cold all night, while I was surprisingly comfortable. Eventually we discovered her sleeping pad was the culprit, underrated, and under-insulated. Gear has come a long way in the forty years I've been camping.

Later in the day, we stopped at a gas station, synonymous with grocery store in this remote area, and bought tortillas, cheese, chips, an apple, and a bag-o-salad for $0.49 because it expired today. Easy on the bikepacking budget, a balance to the unplanned indoor accommodations.

We reached Big Springs before 4 p.m., early enough to wash ourselves and our bike shorts, have dinner and engage in a detailed planning session. Tomorrow, we leave the river and head east into Wyoming, and the next six days promise plenty of bears and very few resupply options.

The day's riding had carried us through expansive rangeland framed by distant mountains. Henry's Fork River begins here, fed by springs pouring straight out of the ground, an impressive 400,000 gallons a day. Before settling in, we walked to see the springs and Johnny Sack's historic cabin. A female moose and her twins fed in the headwaters, their silhouettes reflected in the clear water. It was a reminder that sometimes the best moments arrive quietly, long after the corn dog glory has faded.

Our problem of the day—Tara had a minor rack issue earlier, a loose screw, the same problem I'd had two days ago. Maybe everyone biking for weeks or months at a time has a screw loose.

Chapter 7: The People Who Carry Us

How many people do we need to feel whole?

I've come to believe that a life isn't built from a single great love or a single great friendship, but from a constellation of people, each illuminating a different part of who we are. I never set out to collect so many relationships, but on the trail along the miles and mountains of life, I found myself surrounded by a husband, two boyfriends, a handful of fierce women, a tribe of runners and rescuers, and a sprawling family. Each one fills a space in me that no one else could. Fulfillment, it turns out, isn't a fixed point. It shifts, expands, asks us to keep growing.

John is my anchor, the balanced presence who knows the long arc of my life. Harold and Roger are my emotional companions, men I love in a way that has nothing to do with sex and everything to do with trust, adventure, and the quiet understanding that comes from shared experience.

I once sat in a pedicure chair with Nancy, Harold's wife and my closest friend, while the pedicurists tried to untangle our relationships. We told them Harold was my boyfriend. The joke didn't translate, but we laughed anyway. Our lives have never fit into tidy boxes, and we've stopped trying to make them look that way.

Nancy is blunt in a way that feels like relief—no guessing, no subtext, just the truth handed to you clean. She says she wants to want adventure, but she's honest enough to admit she'd rather read about it from her armchair. What she does want is sun, straight talk, and a friendship that doesn't require costume changes. Sitting beside her, feet in warm water, I felt that rare comfort of being fully known and not needing to explain a thing.

Roger can no longer ride his bike. Parkinson's has taken that from him, along with pieces of the man he once was—an avid climber, a lover of wild places. His wife, Annie, is a force of nature, caring for him with a strength I don't possess. Being with them reminds me that adventure isn't always a summit; sometimes it's simply stepping outside.

Harold is cut from Adirondack granite, craggy, quick to laugh, and full of stories I had to learn not to believe. We once spent a week trapping beaver in the Adirondacks, breaking ice on the ponds and trudging through early snow. He's likely one of the last true trappers up there. When the market for pelts disappeared, he continued to trap the problem beavers causing flooding on his land. One year her trapped fourteen beavers and left their carcasses for the black bears. Every morning he left the beavers he'd caught and the following morning there were always gone. Even bears have to eat. Annually now we spend time fishing together.

And then there's Paula. At seventy-four she lives alone on her mountain, not as a remnant of the life she shared with Al, but as the architect of the one she's had to rebuild since his passing. When the outdoor furnace died, she didn't surrender to the cold; she re-engineered her entire off-grid system, swapping out what she couldn't maintain alone and reinforcing what she could. She chases off porcupines and the men who try to explain her own life back to her, both with the same unblinking determination.

Her life changed with Al's passing, but she didn't. She stayed defiant, independent, and unwilling to be underestimated. She's learning to accept help from neighbors, but only on her terms—never as charity, always as collaboration.

What defines Paula is the way she keeps adapting that mountain life so she can stay exactly where she chooses to be. And a true friend forces you to look at your worst self, or your unlived self, and keep moving toward the life you want. She does that for me.

My intermittent help—stacking wood, shoveling snow—feels small compared to what she gives me. She forces me to look inward, to examine the life I'm living instead of just moving through it.

There are so many others, and I am grateful for everyone who comes into my life, for a season or a lifetime. Together, they form the constellation that makes me whole.

Blixen and Una Have a Bath

Day 25—Saturday, September 10
36.4 miles today • 940.67 miles total
To Warm River Campground

It has been twenty-five days since we started riding the Great Divide, and we've covered 940 miles so far. Should I note that we have not had even one full rest day? Stop the whining! This morning, the moose from last night browsed next to our campsite as we ate breakfast. I heard a loud thump and looked around with trepidation, hoping it wasn't a grizzly. A few minutes later, after quietly scanning the area, it became clear the thud was the large brown female moose lying down in the grass about twenty yards away.

It was cold again, about 24°F. We started with toe warmers in our cycling shoes, full rain gear, hats under helmets, and mittens over cycling gloves. As the sun rose, so did the temperature, and soon it was a comfortable 50°F.

Warm River Campground is considered one of the nicest forest service sites on the trail and it is stunning. The river winds through the campground, with flat tent sites along the banks. Fly fishermen dot the water. The river is sparkling, clear, and cold, not warm as the name implies. Everything is relative: in mid-winter it might feel warm, but in late summer it was cold enough for Jon's testicles to fully retract during his bath, or so he claimed.

We arrived mid-afternoon and washed ourselves, our clothes, and our bikes in the river. Blixen and Una were full of grit and grime, grinding and clunking with every pedal stroke. Lois's bike was cranky too. All three were thrilled to be scrubbed clean. As was Jon.

Today's ride took us through a drive-through coffee shop (a highlight) and across flat and downhill terrain, partly on a rail trail. We followed a side road for a bit because the main trail had volcanic sand-filled potholes and deep sandy patches that swallowed our tires. Jon and Lois, with their fatter tires, had an easier time.

We saw a lot of bear scat again as we descended through Bear Gulch. At one point we passed an old, abandoned mining tunnel. Debris from the collapsed tunnel forced the trail to detour high above the river along a bluff with spectacular views.

The river flowed powerfully to our left. Overhead, a large raptor carried a good-sized fish in its talons. I couldn't confidently identify the bird, maybe a red-tailed hawk. We ran the gauntlet of a few cows in our path, but overall, it was a fun day, pure Type I fun: comfortable riding, nice weather, and a simple focus on life's essentials: food and shelter. This was the kind of day I envisioned at home while planning this trip. A simple day, with no complications.

Tomorrow, we cross from Idaho into Wyoming and begin to see the Tetons. The goal tomorrow is to reach Colter Bay. Then four days on the trail before the next town.

Early to bed. Tomorrow is anticipated to be a high-mileage day.

The Princess and the Pea

Day 26—Sunday, September 11
62.7 miles today • 1003.37 miles total
To Colter Bay

We knew it would be a long day, so we were up at 6 a.m. with frost thick on the tents. I hadn't slept much; there was something under my sleeping mat creating a lump. A root, perhaps. Or a pea. And I am, apparently, a princess. We were on our bikes just after 7:30 a.m.

Maybe it was that lump under my mat, or the cold that seeped into my bones, but in those early miles I found myself thinking about the job that returned me to New Hampshire from New York. A place where the discomfort wasn't physical, it was moral.

> On my very first day at the new job, my new boss, the owner, opened a management meeting by announcing he wanted to fire someone. His tone was full of disgust, bitterness,

and something darker. I remember thinking, *Uh oh. I don't belong here.* But I stayed, because that's what I'd always done, tolerated the pea under the mattress and told myself it wasn't that bad.

It only got stranger. My marketing team once completed every task he'd assigned—a fireman for a trade show, a rebranding review, a new sales deck—and he turned red with anger. "You weren't supposed to execute my grandiose ideas," he sputtered. I told him, as calmly as I could, that he needed to differentiate between "grandiose ideas" and assignments. He didn't appreciate the feedback.

One of my teammates whispered the survival strategy: "Don't do anything he asks the first time. He's probably asked two other people already. He doesn't want it done. If he asks you a third time, consider it, but check with others first." It was ludicrous and unsustainable, a workplace version of sleeping on a rock and pretending it's fine.

After three months, I took him to lunch and I offered my resignation. I told him I couldn't represent him, couldn't work in an environment where people were starved of respect, and sometimes starved literally, through six-hour meetings with no lunch. The no lunch break was my line in the sand, with my hummingbird metabolism.

He asked me to stay, promised me a promotion to President and a significant raise, but the truth was already clear. I didn't belong there. I was enticed into staying by higher pay and a request to provide "coaching" on his behavior. Imagine providing your boss feedback on his lack of manners. I never did voluntarily act on my conviction to leave, but a couple of years later, we were sold to a venture capital firm. As is not atypical in this type of transaction, management is sometimes "let go". As President, my position was terminated and I recall the event clearly. Sitting at a conference room table with the owner and human resources, I felt my shoulders physically rise two inches on hearing the news of my termination. Perhaps I should have stayed true to my convictions, listened to that part of myself that had known it from day one.

Maybe that's why the pea under my sleeping mat bothered me so much. I've spent too many years ignoring discomfort I should have paid attention to and reacted to. Out here, on the trail, I'm learning to trust the signals, whether it's a cold morning, a lump under my tent, or the quiet voice that says, *this isn't right.*

I've also learned to appreciate the benefits and personal growth of all my employment experiences. This one had delivered some very close friends.

I know this is repetitive, but today WAS the coldest morning yet. Temperatures continue to drop as summer ends and fall approaches, and I may be in denial because I do not like the cold. Like the hikers in the White Mountains who need rescuing because it "unexpectedly gets dark every day," I am dismayed that it is "unexpectedly getting colder each day" as fall deepens.

We started with a paved climb, which helped warm us. Then we turned onto Robinson Creek Road, then Ashton Flagg Road, and eventually into Grizzly Gulch. Immediately after the sign announcing we were in Grizzly Gulch, we saw three very large piles of grizzly scat, fresh. Jon, who had commented on the size of the bear relative to the size of the scat the day before, said nothing this time. He just pedaled faster. He's fully cognizant of the fact that he doesn't have to ride faster than the bear, just faster than us.

The dirt road was bumpy and challenging. Eventually a big truck barreled toward us, dragging a dust cloud behind it like Pig Pen from the Snoopy comics. We all stopped to hold our breath. The young man driving also stopped abruptly. He turned out to be the sag wagon for three guys on cross country motorcycles. He offered us water, Dr Pepper, granola bars, anything he had. At first, we declined, but Jon has since reprimanded us and taught us to accept all offerings of food, even if we don't want them, because he will eat them. Was this the first day I realized his pants were falling off?

The young man, also named John, had five huge truck tires in the back of his pickup, all with plugs in them. "Hazard of running sag wagon on these roads," he said. "Lots of flat tires." He was backtracking to look for the cover to one of the motorcycle toolboxes. I'm quite sure I saw that cover, about fourteen inches long, four inches wide, twenty miles back. If I picked up all the parts and debris we've passed on the trail, I could build a vehicle. He was kind, generous, and a reminder that the people you meet along the way add so much color to the adventure.

When the miles got quiet, someone always seemed to appear, an easy reminder that this ride, like life, is made of brief crossings and shared moments, a small reminder that our stories overlap more than we think.

Throughout the day we stopped to pump water from streams. Lunch, as usual, was my slump, five hours in, exhausted and hungry, but I always recover. But I was growing even thinner.

Later, many miles in, on a very rough dirt road, we came upon a camper towing a car. A 30-foot rig, creeping along at five miles an hour, weaving in and out of ruts and potholes. Madness. Like what we are doing is not a different form of madness.

We passed thickets of huckleberries, scouting for bears each time. Huckleberries look like blueberries but are quite sour. We also saw a couple of pickup trucks gathering firewood from public lands, allowed in some places, prohibited in others.

We arrived in the Tetons late in the day after nine hours pedaling the bikes and more than eleven hours of travel time. We stopped for pizza on Jackson Lake before riding the last two miles into Colter Bay. The campground has over 300 sites and was completely booked, but cyclists and backpackers get their own designated area, expansive, quiet, and nearly empty.

It was a cold night. We went to bed with no specific plans for the next day, deciding to gauge our level of exhaustion in the morning.

Sallies, Not Tough ~~as Indians~~

Day 27—Monday, September 12
18.9 miles today • 1022.27 miles total
To Hatchet Resort

Today felt like we were being "soft." Another night spent in comfort. As a child, we called each other "sally" when we were being wimpy and revered being thought of as an "Indian" when we were "tough".

Writing this book has made me more aware of the assumptions I carried without noticing—how easily we repeat old phrases without thinking about the weight they hold. The world has moved on from those expressions, and rightly so. My admiration isn't for a stereotype; it's for the real resilience people show in their own lives. The old compliment about being "tough as an Indian" belongs to another time. What I mean is that I'm in awe of anyone's resilience and fortitude. And that was not us today.

The Tetons were thick with grizzlies, and we woke around 7 a.m. but didn't leave camp until closer to 9 a.m. Elk had bugled through the night, that magical, flute-like call echoing across the dark.

> The first time I heard elk bugling was with my youngest sister in Yellowstone, not far from here. We were celebrating her college graduation with a backpacking trip. After watching the mandatory bear safety video, we hiked into the backcountry and set up camp. When the bugling started, I had no idea what creature made that sound. The howling we also heard, I was sure, was wolves.
>
> Jess was awake and shivering.
>
> "Are you cold?" I whispered.
>
> "No. I'm scared."
>
> It hadn't occurred to me to be scared. But I remembered meeting hikers in New Hampshire earlier that year, a father and his young daughter staring wide, eyed at a pond. A bullfrog croaked its deep "jug-o-rum," and they asked, "What is THAT?" I was polite but, in my mind I had been disdainful that they didn't recognize a frog. Now, lying in a field listening to the unfamiliar vocalizations of elk, I was humbled. We are only familiar with our own small environments.
>
> At first light, Jess shot out of the tent, her fear evaporated.

"Where are you going?" I asked.

"I'm going to get eaten by a monster or poop my pants, and I do not want to poop my pants out here."

That is one way to overcome fear.

Later, in the pay shower at the campground, I moaned in pleasure at being clean and embarrassed her thoroughly.

In the morning, we pedaled a couple of miles into Colter Bay proper for groceries and showers. Five dollars per shower, but worth every penny to be warm and clean. We stocked up for the next three or four days, our stretch to Pinedale, Wyoming, and spread everything out in front of the store to repack our bikes. We researched lodging options for the night, calling every place within fifty-six miles, and found a teepee for $15 each. With the high density of grizzlies, we wanted a public place to stay.

The ride was relatively flat. Traffic increased as we approached a parking area and suddenly park rangers and bear rangers were waving people back. Volunteers in official garb appeared, these are the "bear brigade," who show up to manage the crowd when a collared bear is sighted. Grizzly #399 was just down the bank, heading toward the road. She may have had a cub with her. Rangers urged everyone to get back into their vehicles.

We didn't stick around. We had no vehicle to retreat into, and prudence won.

We didn't know it then, but Grizzly #399 was a legend, born in Pilgrim Creek in 1996, collared in 2001, and mother to eight litters and eighteen known cubs. She roamed hundreds of miles across Grand Teton National Park and the Bridger-Teton National Forest. While writing this book, I learned she had been fatally struck by a vehicle in Snake River Canyon at age twenty-eight. She starred in her own PBS documentary, *Grizzly 399: Queen of the Tetons*. Her ashes were returned to Pilgrim Creek, her birthplace.

After leaving the bear jam, we stopped at the post office to mail postcards and then at every convenience store, all two of them, searching desperately for additional hand and foot warmers. We found exactly none. I was anxious. Being cold drains my energy, and the temperatures were dropping fast. Unlike Bear #399, I am not covered in fur and have very little fat on my bones.

Can I really do this? The thought does creep into my mind occasionally, particularly when I am cold or fearing the cold. I'm cold, tired, hungry, and living on junk food. We're not even half-way. I've always feared dying of hypothermia, freezing to death in the wild. We'd used up all our warmers, and I worried about the next few days.

I probably come across as self-confident. My parents instilled a "can do" attitude in us, and I'm grateful for that. But this adventure has exposed my insecurities. It's easy to be confident when you're not the weakest link. When I adventure with people who are slower or less strong, I never mind waiting. But when *I* am the slowest, anxiety creeps in. I worry about keeping up, push harder, become inefficient, and slow down even more. Fatigue feeds the spiral.

Today was short, just under twenty miles, a rest day before another big push tomorrow. When we arrived at the teepee we had reserved, it was… not stellar. Grungy, unswept, no way to close or secure the door, and nowhere to store food except inside with us, a guaranteed bear attractant. Each of us stepped inside, looked around, and made a derogatory comment.

We splurged on a condo room on the same property, more for bear safety than comfort. Yeah, right.

We enjoyed the luxury of two showers in one day, compensation for the next four days, when we'll likely be bathing in a creek, or *crik*, as they say here, if we bathe at all.

We ended the day in the restaurant with burgers, fries, and hopes for a warmer start in the morning.

Do NOT stop for bears

Day 28 - Tuesday, September 13
44 miles today • 1,066.27 total, 4,347 feet of climbing
To Crooked Creek Cabin

The electronic road signs warned us not to stop for bears. "Stay in your vehicle," they said, in flashing yellow lights. Our "vehicles" offered all the protection of a paper bag, but by now, we were starting to be conditioned to bear warnings and bears, just another part of the scenery. I hope they continue to mind their own business as we mind ours.

This morning, I realized I'd forgotten to thank Jon, in yesterday's blog post, for all his mechanical help, changing Tara's brake pads, adjusting my shifter, patiently explaining the brake lever barrel adjuster. I work on my bike, but not frequently or repetitively enough to have full confidence. I still can't remember which barrel adjustment direction tightens the cable, and resort to trial and error every time, but Jon knows, and that is a benefit of traveling companions with various skill sets. Gratitude felt like a small anchor on a day that promised bears.

We climbed Togwotee Pass to 9,600 feet and stopped for lunch at a tourist pullout. A truck pulled in and the driver leaned out to warn us about three grizzlies, just 100 yards away. A mother and two cubs. Gulp. We didn't see them, but the knowledge of their proximity caused us to question the routing options ahead of us.

There was an optional dirt road, the official Tour Divide route, but it was remote and quiet and exactly the kind of place a bear might prefer to dine. We chose the main road instead. Our reasons were many: Tara's wheel was cracking, we wanted a smoother approach to the final seven-mile grind, we hoped for vehicular assistance if needed, and, in case it wasn't clear, bears. Fear wasn't dictating our choices, but it was definitely part of the conversation. After twenty-five miles of climbing, we went down, fast, and I was grateful for every passing car that felt like a potential witness if things went sideways.

As we pedaled, I found myself thinking of another time I felt exposed, years ago, standing in a conference room where I was supposed to be the expert but felt like prey. Fear has a way of shrinking the world, whether it's a bear or a boardroom. Back then, I learned that preparation, not bravado, was what kept me afloat. That same lesson was echoing now: you don't outrun fear, you learn to move with it. Make informed decisions, have confidence in your knowledge, be flexible, be prudent.

We stopped at Togwotee Mountain Lodge and then Lava Mountain Resort in a desperate hunt for hand-warmers. Success at the second stop eased my anxiety about cold hands and feet. When we have plenty of inventory, we use them prophylactically, tiny insurance policies tucked into our shoes. The weather was turning colder, and inventory helps to keep some of the anxiety at bay.

The last seven miles up Union Pass Road were a ninety-minute grind. We reached Crooked Creek Cabin at over 8,000 feet, still ten miles from the actual summit. As we approached, a large white dog with porcupine quills in his nose greeted us with a few half-hearted growls. Even the dogs out here had stories. My heart ached for him. We booked a room, cooked dinner on the porch, and watched the sky darken with the promise of wet days ahead.

Lying in my sleeping bag that night, I realized something had shifted. The fear that had shadowed the day hadn't disappeared, but it had softened. It had become something I could acknowledge without letting it take the wheel. I wasn't fearless by the time we reached Crooked Creek Cabin, but I was humbly confident. Fear is healthy and our fears were now something we could comfortably carry or leave at the roadside on our detours.

There are days on the Divide when the trail feels almost meditative, long, open stretches where the miles unspool without urgency and your mind finally has space to roam. Or long, slow uphill climbs, steady progress toward the intended destination. No drama, no weather tantrums, no mechanical mutiny. Just the steady rhythm of breath and pedal stroke, the kind of days, flat or hilly, that invites reflection whether you asked for it or not.

Months later, after the Divide was behind me, I would think back to these quiet, disciplined miles when Leigh was preparing for Ironman Arizona. Not the race itself, but the long runway leading up to it, the anticipation, the logistics, the low-grade hum of nerves that sits under everything when you're getting ready for something big.

I flew to Phoenix to watch her race. Leigh had trained all summer, threading workouts through trips to international destinations, running unfamiliar streets, renting bikes when she could, doing whatever it took to stay on track. She was a brain cancer survivor, a marathoner, and a two-time Half-Ironman finisher, but the full Ironman was a different beast. We all wondered the same thing: after everything her body had endured, could she complete 140.6 miles powered only by her own strength?

Her biggest worry was the swim. The Salt River in Tempe is notoriously cold, and once Leigh gets chilled, her drive evaporates. The day before the race, she decided to slip into the water just long enough to feel it. We poured warm water down the front of her wetsuit, a trick learned from a race clinic, and she joined the line of athletes. She swam a short loop, climbed out, and said, "That wasn't too bad."

I hadn't realized I'd been holding my breath until that moment. She wasn't rattled. She wasn't defeated. The fear was still there, but it wasn't steering the ship.

Out on the Divide, pedaling up or through those long monotonous stretches, I felt the echo of that same fragile hope, the way preparation and fear can sit side by side without canceling each other out. Leigh had done everything she could. I had done the same. And sometimes that has to be enough.

Fortune Favors the Brave

Day 29 - Wednesday, September 14
42 miles today • 1,108 miles total
To Whiskey Grove near Whiskey Creek

We left Crooked Creek Cabin bundled in every scrap of rain gear we owned, dog poop bags on our hands and feet, "bin liners" over our rain jackets (Lois's British touch), helmet covers, shoe covers, rain pants, rain jackets, and the precious hand and toe warmers we'd finally found the day before. After two nights in a real bed and weeks of good weather, the forecast had turned. Wyoming had decided to get wet.

The drizzle began almost immediately. Climbing Union Pass while being simultaneously hot and cold is its own brand of absurdity—windy, wet, gritty, gravel sticking to everything. The climb stretched for ten miles on dirt, with the occasional truck, camper, or four-wheeler passing by. Most people were courteous. We passed a few white canvas hunting tents with stovepipes poking through the roofs. In our soggy desperation, the thought of stepping into one of those warm tents was almost too tempting, but we knew a snowmobile safety cabin was a few miles ahead.

As Brad, my niece's husband, told me before I left: *embrace the suck.*

So, we did. We stopped whenever anyone needed to, for food, clothing adjustments, or morale checks. Our group of four is good at reading each other, good at preventing a suffer-fest before it starts. For me, the "suck" wasn't too bad thanks to the warmers tucked into my gloves and shoes.

At 17.5 miles, we reached the Strawberry Safety Cabin. We were cold, wet, and a little defeated. Jon and Tara got a fire going, and soon we were steaming like horses after a hard ride. Tara was soaked through. We melted cheese sandwiches on the woodstove and ate them like they were gourmet. Warmth, food, and dryness were luxuries that felt extravagant.

Outside, the sky couldn't make up its mind. Dark, almost black clouds. Then a brief blue "sucker hole", the kind that tricks you into thinking the weather is clearing, only to slam shut again. On some adventures, we rejoice over a "sucker hole", using it as the motivation to "get back out there" even though we know it is a trick of the heavens. Lois spotted a bald eagle perched across the meadow. Inside, we were warm, dry, full, and dangerously sleepy.

We made a deal: if it wasn't raining at 3 p.m., we'd push on for the remaining twenty-four miles. At three p.m., the sky held. As we rolled away, Jon said, "Fortune favors the brave." I countered with my brother Nick's wisdom: "If you're going to be dumb, you have to be tough." We wondered which category we'd fall into over the next four hours, fortunate or dumb and tough?

A few miles down the muddy road, a man in a truck stopped to warn us about a large boar grizzly ahead. That always gets our attention. Most of the group sang loudly. My singing has not improved on this trip, still can't carry a tune in a pannier, so I just yelled out fragments of "100 Bottles of Beer on the Wall" whenever the silence felt too big.

Ben, our navigation app, promised an afternoon of downhill. The terrain disagreed, with rolling hills, as many ups as downs. Normally that mismatch demoralizes me, but today the climbs kept me warm. This side of the pass had clearly been drenched; puddles and mud everywhere.

Near the campground, another man in a truck stopped and handed Jon a Sprite. Jon accepted immediately, he's gotten so thin he literally can't keep his pants up now, and calories are critical out here. He and Lois have both had to take in their waistbands.

We reached Whiskey Grove around 7 p.m. A camper van pulled out as we arrived, leaving the entire campground empty. Not exactly comforting in bear country. But we'd stayed dry, and we were closer to town, closer to the bike shop, the grocery store, and the sporting goods store.

Fortune favored the brave today. Or maybe the dumb. Either way, we made it. Is today the day to quit? I think not.

It was my mom's birthday today, and I missed her. Adventure has its costs, and this was one of them.

No Bears Allowed South of Pinedale

Day 30—Thursday September 15
36+ miles today •1,144 miles total
To Pinedale, Wyoming

Last night we cooked in the campsite *across* the road from where we slept, because nothing says "peaceful night under the stars" like relocating your entire kitchen to avoid becoming a bear's midnight charcuterie board. We stripped off our "cooking clothes," stuffed them into the bear box with the food, and did our nightly ritual of checking every bike bag for forgotten snacks. I've been woken more than once by a rustle outside, heart pounding, convinced a grizzly is out there sniffing for a rogue cookie crumb I missed.

We're almost to the magical line where "they" say grizzlies don't go any farther south. But who are *they*, and did anyone send the bears a memo? In the dark, I swear I heard one - snap! crack! the sound of something large and carnivorous stepping on a stick. I lay there clutching my bear spray, contemplating my role as potential prey. It's humbling and I am grateful those thoughts don't visit often. In most places, humans are at the top of the food chain. Out here, we're basically burritos with opinions.

Morning arrived heavy and damp. Everything was soaked, the tents, the air, the ground, our spirits. Getting out of a warm sleeping bag felt like a betrayal of everything good in the world. But once one person unzips their tent, the rest of us follow. There's only so much time to pack, eat, and dress before you're either too cold to function or the posse rolls on without you.

We were on the road by 9 a.m., pedaling through fog thick enough to qualify as a weather-based personality test.

Lois, the realist, notes that fog is just weather doing its job and keeps pedaling.

Tara, the worrier, wonders what wildlife is lurking ten feet off the shoulder.

Jon, the stoic, treats it like another item on the day's menu: fog, gravel, miles.

And me, forever the optimist, assuming the sun is "right there" behind the gray curtain.

The ride into Pinedale was easy by Divide standards, not too hilly, and took about four hours. We saw our first antelope and two Sandhill cranes. The cranes were tall, elegant, and sporting bright red crowns, like they were dressed for a gala we were not invited to.

In Pinedale, Tara picked up her new rear wheel at the bike shop. The mechanics, who've seen every possible GDMBR catastrophe, gave both our bikes a full spa treatment: new chains, brakes, shifter cables. Austin, one of the mechanics, even sold Tara a bike bag off his own bike after hers burst a seam. That's excellent customer service.

We made the rounds: hardware store for more toe warmers, lunch at the brew pub, gear shops, laundry, and food resupply. Ahead lies the Great Basin, a place that looms large in the mythology of this ride.

The Basin is vast, open, and intimidating. Rugged, remote, desolate. Rolling hills, sagebrush, dirt roads, and wind, always wind. Human presence is minimal, giving the place a strange mix of solitude and wilderness. Its beauty lies in the endless sky and the raw, untamed landscape. It's peaceful and demanding, like nature's version of a strict but fair schoolteacher. We'll need four days of food to cross it. I am trying not to stress over it.

Tonight, we're at the Jackalope Inn, a hiker hostel/motel, and I'm thrilled to be inside as thunder, lightning, and rain hammer down. A shout-out to Larry and Austin at Bison Bikes, excellent mechanics, excellent humans.

We explored the hiker box near the laundry machines, where travelers leave unwanted gear. Louis scored a shirt. I ditched my bear spray, good riddance to a few more ounces, though Tara kept hers. She still fears the bears; I fear the weight of the can more than the bears themselves. If a grizzly wants me, have me. I have had a good life and I doubt the extra eleven ounces of pepper spray will make or break the situation.

We did laundry out back and hung our tents on the clothesline to dry once the rain let up. They were still soaked from last night, but at least *we're* dry, warm, and sheltered. Tomorrow, the Great Basin awaits, and I'm sure it has opinions about us too.

Is today the day to quit? Not yet.

Bad Water

Day 31 - Friday, September 16
53.8 miles today • 1198.37 miles total
To Forest Service campsite, Lander Creek, Wyoming

It was wet and soggy when we woke, the kind of morning where everything feels heavier than it should, considering we did not wake in our tents. The four of us went out for breakfast in Pinedale, and not a crumb survived on any plate. As we packed up at the Jackalope Inn, going in and out of the room, our bikes on the hotel curbing, I noticed a freshly killed deer lying on the shoulder across the road. Minutes later, a middle-aged woman appeared with a very large knife and began skinning it. Unexpected, even for Wyoming. Stranger still, the carcass looked almost untouched afterward. Odd.

We lingered around the inn's gas firepit, warming our hands in the drizzle, and didn't roll out until around 11 a.m. A few quick stops included the post office, grocery store, and a drugstore for a prescription. At the bike shop the prior afternoon, we met up with a young couple, Moe and Harry, who turned out to live about an hour from Jon and Lois in British Columbia. Small world. They joined us for the day's ride. They are young and FAST.

The first ten miles were wet and chilly, but the skies eventually dried. The views opened wide, Wyoming echoing Montana in its vastness. By evening we were camping in a cow pasture, cows mooing their commentary. The last few miles had been rolling, with clouds piling behind us like a storm we'd barely outrun.

My derailleur refused to shift into first gear at times, which was maddening, and Tara's pannier clip snapped. Zip ties saved the day. Dinner was chilly and windy, eaten in a field dotted with cow pies. Pumping water was an exercise in desperation: standing on a slope at the creek's edge, trying not to step *in* the cow pies (a losing battle), stretching our water filter hoses to the center of the creek, as far as our arms could reach to avoid the worst of the muck. The creek was only four or five feet wide, so the "center" was not far from the cow dung, relatively speaking.

We boiled the water longer than usual, hoping to avoid giardia, but we needed water and didn't have any other choices regarding an alternative source. My years on a search and rescue team taught me that dehydration increases the risk of hypothermia. Tonight's menu of risks: contaminated water, dehydration, or hypothermia. Choose your adventure.

Still, this was type II fun, miserable in the moment, memorable later. The rock formations around us looked like Joshua Tree, stirring old adventure memories. By 8:15 p.m., all six of us were in our sleeping bags, trying to warm our feet.

> Years before this trip, I learned the hard way what happens when you ignore discomfort for too long. After months of chaos at the mill, unpaid vendors, raw materials running out, payroll hanging by a thread, I finally reached the point where I couldn't pretend anymore.
>
> I called my boss and said, "I am resigning."
>
> He called back later in the day and said, "We will give you a $10,000 raise to stay."
>
> With what money, I wondered, as I held a paycheck I couldn't cash.
>
> "Give the raise to Nancy," I said. "I'm leaving."
>
> Only after I left did I learn that our health insurance hadn't been paid. A hospital bill arrived for a procedure I'd had done, $300 more than it should have been, as medical costs are higher when you are uninsured. Another small betrayal in a long line of them.
>
> It was the first time I walked away not because I wanted to, but because staying meant abandoning myself. I should have listened sooner. I should have trusted the discomfort. But I didn't, not until the real situation became undeniable.

Out here on the trail, I'm finally learning to really listen to those signals, and to act in the moment.

We are finding more of our people, those who take joy in the hardship the Divide offers, who see adversity not as punishment but as a chance to test their steadiness and humor.

Badder Water!

Day 32—Saturday September 17
44.09 miles • 1242.46 miles total
To Sweetwater River, Wyoming

We woke to a hard, beautiful, frosty world. Our tents, bikes, and bags were coated in a thick layer of frost and ice, and we hopped around trying to stay warm. Hand and foot warmers were both compulsory today. We didn't leave camp until just after 9 a.m.

The morning brought rolling hills and mud, the kind that forces you to stay in the parallel tracks or risk sinking into the softening ground. Early on, Jon stepped straight into a puddle and filled his shoe with water. Thank goodness for extra dry socks and doggie bags. As kids, my family used bread bags inside our boots in winter and they work equally as well inside biking shoes. Bags or plastic wrap make a surprising difference in warmth.

We passed through Atlantic City, population fifty-seven, elevation 7,675 feet. I commented that these days felt harder, and Tara pointed out the obvious: we'd just resupplied with four days of food. Heavier bikes, heavier legs. I hadn't made the connection, but she was right. My sorest days always followed a big food haul.

We rode as a group again, Moe and Harry still with us. Young, strong, fast, and delightful. They seemed to enjoy the company, even if we were the "old, slow" contingent.

Lunch was tucked into warm rocks in the sun, again reminding me of Joshua Tree and a February climbing trip where the rock's warmth was welcome. We stopped for water at South Pass City and wandered through the ghost town. Our next off the bikes stop was Wild Bill's place—guns, knives, septic pumping, and a couple of rooms to rent. Out here, you need multiple income streams to survive financially and Bill had it figured out. Trail resources indicated he was the man to ask about crossing the Great Basin, 130 miles of desert with only two water sources. Like the Appalachian Trail, the GDMBR has its own communication network: online posts, Facebook groups, and passing riders. Some stories are fiction, some fact, but Wild Bill's advice was solid.

He told us the winds were calm enough to cross now, but only for two days. We needed to be out of the Basin before day three, when the wind would pick up. We trusted him.

After leaving Wild Bill's, we climbed to an overlook for our first glimpse of the Basin. Vast. Intimidating. Beautiful. Barren.

We camped beside the Sweetwater River, which was anything but sweet. A large beaver swam by, and the remains of game animals, likely birds, floated downstream from where hunters had cleaned their kills. It was the sketchiest water source yet, worse than the cow-pie creek. Thankfully, Tara and I had filtered some water earlier in the day. Mo and Harry would suffer later.

As we set up camp, clouds and wind rolled in, then cleared, leaving a surprisingly pleasant evening by the river, despite its contents. Tomorrow, we enter the feared Great Basin.

Gulp.

I am not dead yet

Day 33 - Sunday, September 18
69.2 miles today • 1311.66 total
To A&M Reservoir

We began our crossing of The Great Basin, 130 miles of sagebrush desert so empty that even FedEx and UPS, normally omnipresent on these backroads, don't bother with it. The only vehicles we saw were a few hunters, one skinning an antelope in the back of his truck, and a couple of oil trucks rumbling between the two depots out here. It felt like riding across the country's abandoned backyard.

We were grateful to have Harry and Jon pulling us through the wind for part of the day. Eventually we turned a corner and caught a tailwind, though the road turned to washboard and rattled us all the way to the remote reservoir campsite.

By late afternoon I had fallen behind, Tara trailing with me, she out of kindness, me out of sheer exhaustion. When we finally rolled in, our friends were chatting with a pair of hikers who handed each of us a banana, some water, and a Werther's candy. Out here, calories are currency, and every edible item feels like a blessing.

Mo, buzzing with energy, told the hikers, "It was a great and easy day!"

I thought, *WHAT?! EASY?!* I'm surely going to die on this adventure.

Difficulty is personal - shaped by age, fitness, experience, and whatever stubbornness you woke up with that morning. At their pace, they were basically on a rolling coffee break. I was at the far reaches of my ability, hauling nonstop for hours and seriously questioning if I could continue at this pace. Still, we were grateful for their pulls through the wind.

And in that exhaustion, the rattling washboard, the endless sage, the wind that felt like it was scraping me clean, something in me opened. The Basin has a way of doing that. It strips away everything unnecessary until you're left with the questions you've been avoiding.

At one point in my professional career, I went through a period where I felt hollowed out by striving. I no longer wanted promotions or titles or the next rung on a ladder I wasn't sure I believed in. Without children, without the structure of a career I trusted, I found myself asking the oldest questions: *Why am I here? What is the point? Who am I becoming?*

For years I'd been drawn to the idea of a Vision Quest, the ancient pattern of stepping away from ordinary life, sitting alone with yourself, and returning changed. The traditional version terrified me: fasting in the desert with nothing but water and your own thoughts. My metabolism is closer to a hummingbird's than a mystic's and I thought that might be a sure way to die unintentionally. But the longing was real.

So, I did a gentler version, guided by my friend Becca. She smudged me with incense, brushed air over me with an eagle feather, and sent me into the woods alone with my questions. I lay in a red bivy bag, dozing, when a hawk circled overhead. It dipped lower and lower, clearly assessing whether I was alive.

"I'm not dead yet," I said out loud, half to the hawk, half to myself.

And something in me knew the path forward: *Keep choosing the life you want.*

At the time, John and I were in a rough patch. He had moved to Maine, living in our cottage, and I was still in New Hampshire, tethered to the place I loved and a job that drained me. I wanted a different life, one outdoors, one with meaning, one where I didn't have to pretend. Watching a small bird build a nest later that day, I had a quiet realization: *You can make a home anywhere.* Nature does it without hesitation. So could I. I wanted to stay in New Hampshire, but John wanted gentler winters and to return to our roots, and family, in Maine.

That Vision Quest didn't give me visions or answers. But it gave me permission. Permission to want more. Permission to leave what wasn't working. Permission to believe that my life could still change.

And maybe that's why the Basin felt strangely familiar, a place where everything unnecessary fell away, and I was left with the truth I had been circling for years.

Setting up tents in the strong gusts was a challenge, though not as bad as the horror stories we'd heard. We held on while they flapped and we anchored them down. The man-made reservoir shimmered in the evening light, and antelope wandered down to drink. The sunset was spectacular, a reward for surviving the day.

We survive crossing the basin

Day 34—Monday, September 19
56.4 miles today • 1368.06 miles total
To Rawlins

Pronghorn herds circled the reservoir at dawn. When we pumped water, the filters clogged almost instantly. The desert water was thick with sediment and algae and it took real effort to gather enough for breakfast and a full day of riding.

All six of us, Mo, Harry, Jon, Lois, Tara, and me, left together. The night had been dry, so our tents weren't wet, which in bikepacking terms translates directly to "not heavy." Spirits were high. We "smashed it," as our Canadian/British friends say, for the first fifteen miles, riding two-by-two down the dirt road at a near-continuous very speedy clip.

We hit pavement, climbed, descended, then returned to dirt. We passed a uranium mine sitting incongruously beside land designated for raptor conservation. An oxymoron if ever there was one. At the next junction, where pavement resumed, we stopped for lunch. A barrel stood there for hunters to deposit one wing from any bird they'd shot. We joked about tossing in six wings from the sage grouse we shot for dinner. It was our dream...

Then came the headwind.

We climbed what felt like a super highway, big trucks roaring past in both directions. The wind was so fierce we had to pedal hard downhill just to avoid being blown backward. It was demoralizing and ludicrous all at once.

We reached Rawlins and squeezed three tents into one KOA site right beside the highway. KOAs are conveniently located for RVs, which means they're also conveniently located for truck traffic, all night long. The $2 per person fee softened the blow, as did the luxuries: ice cream, showers, flush toilets, washer/dryers.

The wind again made pitching tents difficult, but it dried our laundry in minutes. Town chores followed the usual pattern: cleaning, snacking, and food inventory. After laundry, cleaning our dishes well in a soapy sink, and showers, we rode to a Mexican restaurant. Tara's lips caught fire from the salsa, and tears streamed down her face as she dabbed them with ice. Then we rode another three miles round-trip, in the dark, to Walmart for a resupply, enough food for three or four days to get us to Steamboat Springs. Another state is nearly completed, ridden through from border to border, as we get closer to crossing the Wyoming border into

Colorado. I had left my headlamp back in the tent so the trip back to the KOA was fraught with angst. Fear of crashing, hitting a curb, bumping Tara ahead of me.

By the time we returned to camp, I was completely toasted. Four challenging days in a row, and I could barely see straight. We crawled into our tents and fell asleep to the soundtrack of zooming trucks, air brakes, and highway hum, just background white noise, after the desert silence.

It was a bad day, but no one died

Day 35 - Tuesday, September 20
50.2 miles today • 1418 miles total
To Forest Service Campsite

Mentally this was my most difficult day of the trip to date. We have not taken a full rest day, and it is beginning to feel like we have pressure to keep going and to keep up with others. Before this trip began, I was worried about being slow. Not really about being slow, as I can fully embrace my limitations, but the exhaustion I expected from trying to keep up with someone with a lot more endurance. I laugh that I have the same pace in a 5K or a marathon. Speed and strength are not my strong suits, but endurance at my own pace is surely a strength. Like the Energizer Bunny, but not fast. It is as though we have some unmentioned deadline. We do, sort of.

All 50 miles today were into a brutal headwind, and we had to pedal both up and *down* the hills. Tara and I were alone, as I feared I could no longer keep up with the crowd. I felt "at fault" for something not definable. In my mind, I am a bit of a cry-baby. When you are the strongest, as I am on hiking trips, you always think it is easy for everyone. But when you are the one struggling, your mind plays games. As Tara went down one hill she said, "Please, gravity, win this battle with the wind." If SHE was saying that, then I had reason to worry.

We are not complaining though, as we choose to do this and we do love it. We miss our friends and their help in a headwind. Everyone out here has chosen this adventure, and everyone is so stoic, but I am a bit of a fraidy-cat whiner in my mind. I don't know why I am afraid of the hills, because when you get to them, you just go up, for as long as it takes, sometimes hours. Everyone has their battles, and you only become aware of others' demons through advice quietly solicited and quietly shared. Sometimes someone will make an off-hand comment about chafing or pose a question such as "What are the symptoms of giardia?" but never voiced as a complaint. Butt sores, raw crotch, stiff back, sore neck, stomach ailments, rough nights of no sleep, everyone copes quietly and keeps on pedaling. We recognize and acknowledge discomfort is part of the adventure.

Years before this ride, on a crisp fall afternoon in the White Mountains, I was out with the Search and Rescue team. After two days of combing the woods, we were reassigned to a pocket of forest the GPS tracks had somehow skipped. The leaves were mostly down, the air crisp, the terrain steep along a narrow ravine. A dog handler was coming up the valley as we angled down, and we all saw him at the same moment.

He was wearing only shorts. No shirt, no shoes. His skin was so pale it didn't look real, the true definition of alabaster, a word I've never read the same way since. The stillness of him was jarring against a forest so full of life. It was suspected he had taken his own life, based on a text he'd sent a family member before heading into the mountains.

We radioed the SAR captain. The coroner would have to hike in before we could move him, and another teammate would carry in the litter. It would be a long wait.

What surprised me almost as much as the scene itself was how my teammates climbed a small ridge, sat down, and began to eat lunch. "It's going to be a long wait," one said. "We need to stay warm and keep our strength."

I was frozen, but I could feel my body slowly recalibrating, blood returning to my brain, breath evening out. *You signed up for this,* I told myself. *Do what's needed.* So, I sat with them and ate, trying to act as though this were normal. For them, maybe it was. I wondered how many bodies they had seen. I wondered how many I would see.

I'd had my own dark thoughts in life, times when I'd imagined a climbing accident or hypothermia taking me. But standing there in that ravine, looking at a man who had been found too late, I made a quiet promise: I would never put others through this. I would never intentionally create a situation where someone had to search for me, or find me, or carry me out of the woods.

It was the day I understood, in a visceral way, the responsibility we have to the people who might someday come looking.

After a "bad" day on an adventure, we often shrug and laugh, "Well, no one died, right?" It's easy to say that when you've never actually encountered death in the wilderness. I don't say it so lightly anymore. Once you've stood beside a real body in a real search-and-rescue situation, you understand the difference between inconvenience, physical discomfort and tragedy. A tough bike day is just a tough bike day. And truly, we're having some spectacular days.

We are all enjoying the incredible views, the unique perspective of seeing the United States one mile at a time and feeling grateful for the opportunity to be out here. Lois especially has a great attitude, minor ailments come with the adventure. I guess if it was easy, the trail would be crowded.

I am tired after keeping up with the younger folks for four days. Riding today, Tara asked me to explain what was wrong. As a nurse, she was looking for signs and symptoms, and I could only express, "I'm so tired." "I have no other descriptors, I'm tired, full body fatigue." My legs feel spent, so we have planned a full day off in Steamboat Springs, still three days away. She is patient with me, but clearly far more capable of covering more mileage than me.

We listened to the trucks all night cruising on the highway and were up early, around 6 a.m. Some folks thought about sleeping in, and everyone planned a bit later departure to make some phone calls and sort food. Tara and I decided to stay a bit longer in camp to map out the dates to meet Mimi and Larry, who are coming to visit, and to estimate when we will be near our friend Maggie, so we can plan to see her too. We also wanted to drop postcards and some gear at the post office, for ourselves and some packages for our friends, which took us off route a bit.

The other four headed out before us, and we hoped to see them again in Steamboat. But that is the nature of friends on a trip like this. You travel together for days, and then perhaps you don't cross paths again, for many miles, or perhaps never again.

Our day was hard due to the wind, and we could not get to the campsite where the others were headed. Not having the strong young guns pulling us along made us (me) even slower. We stopped for lunch near a cattle guard and talked with a north-bound cyclist. He was quick to talk about his crotch issues. I think Tara exudes "caring nurse" in her interpersonal encounters.

As for critters today, no bears, but we saw a large animal skull on the roadside, a large dead snake, and a rabbit. At one point we deployed the emergency shelter and sat out a ten-minute storm, with loud thunder and lightning. The shelter is great; similar in shape to a parachute, lightweight, warms up quickly, deploys in seconds, and keeps the rain out. After the rain stopped, a beautiful rainbow came out. The cows all around were mooing and mooing. Maybe they did not like the wind either. Or they were on the wrong side of the fence or the wrong side of the cattle guard. You never can tell with those beasts, seemingly complaining at large.

Late in the day, we climbed into the aspen forests from the open scrubland. We rode until after 6 p.m., and I felt as though I was barely moving. The indicated Forest Service site on our map had no water, and we set up our tent right under the deer-hang, or maybe those crossbeams are for a bear bag? But we are out of grizzly country, and Tara says, "Black bears are scaredy bears." The sunset through the trees was a pretty red. It was a bit windy as we retired, and we were camped near some hunters who were up at 5:30 am, headed out on their four wheelers. It is bow season for elk hunting.

We make it to Colorado

Day 36 - Wednesday, September 21
39.7 miles today • 1,457.96 total
To Brush Mountain/Kirsten's Land

We left camp before breakfast because we had no water, always a compelling reason to get moving. A mile or two up the road we found a creek and pumped water with the enthusiasm of people who had already imagined their own dehydration-related obituaries. It was a chilly morning, and without breakfast we were cold and cranky, so we rode uphill until we found sunshine and then stopped to cook. Nothing like oatmeal at altitude to restore the will to live.

The riding was both varied and the same, packed dirt, rolling terrain, and then a paved downhill so steep it felt like a theme-park ride. Or maybe it just felt that way because, for once, the wind wasn't trying to shove us back to Canada.

We left Wyoming and entered Colorado, stopping just before the state line for a snack. The first "town" we reached was Slater, where the post office appeared to be operating out of an abandoned trailer. A bold architectural choice.

As we climbed, we passed two snakes basking in the sun. Then two more. Two were rattlers, the other two were unidentified but definitely slitherers. By the time we reached Brush Mountain Lodge, we'd seen enough reptiles to question our camping plans. *Are we sleeping near this snake convention? Yikes.*

We met Kirsten driving away from the Brush Mountain Lodge, as her season had just ended. She is the legendary lodge keeper and was on her way to Phoenix after closing-up for the season. She handed us two Mountain Dews, gave us directions to a water source near the deck of the lodge, and told us to camp on her land. Rumor had it she was wonderful; rumor was correct. People are astonishingly kind out here.

We filled up at the lodge and chatted with elk hunters who were bow hunting. Then we biked another mile and scouted for a tent site on Kirsten's land, wandering up and down an overgrown road like Goldilocks with panniers. Is this a nice spot? Too bumpy. Is this a nice spot? Too wet. Is this a nice spot? It is not "just right" but will have to suffice. Eventually we pitched the tent on the edge of the road where the land sloped westward. It was going to rain, so we ate dinner at 4:30 p.m. and were zipped inside by five p.m.

It was a long evening. Tara sewed up her vest, which had been caught in her brake and shredded. The result was functional but looked like something Frankenstein might wear to a casual brunch. We laughed hard. I wrote notes for the blog, sorted photos, and ate eight powdered donuts because I am an adult and no one can stop me.

Now we're sticky, stinky, and huddled in the tent with a cup of tea, waiting for the Marsha Rule to kick in. We are not allowed to go to bed before 8 p.m. It's 7:42 and we are suffering.

MUD MUD MUD MUD MUD

If you think you can, you can
If you think you can't, you can't

Day 37 - Thursday, September 22
12.5 miles today • 1,470.46 total
To MUD / Forest Service Site FR 42

Today wins the award for "Most Challenging Day Yet," though not the most difficult, just the muddiest. A distinction I never expected to make in my life.

We packed up early from Kirsten's land, soggy and optimistic, hoping to reach Steamboat. The optimism lasted about seven minutes. Everything was wet. Even my bright yellow sleeping pad ended up with a swath of mud, a stain that will now serve as a lifelong flashback trigger.

Before leaving, we saw a rainbow and took it as a good omen. This was a mistake. It was not.

We quickly hit the infamous peanut-butter mud, thick, sticky, and capable of stopping a bike dead, as if someone had welded your wheels to the earth. We made fewer than six miles in just under five hours. Five. Hours. We needed our friends back.

Every three to five minutes we stopped to scrape mud from the tires, the frame, the shoes, the spokes, and possibly our souls. We used sticks, rocks, and a bike tool. We pushed through sagebrush, cow patties, and cattle trails, sometimes inventing new trails entirely. The thick mud is almost indescribable in its stickiness. After one revolution, the wheels would no longer turn, so caked in mud the wheels did not fit through the frame to spin.

At one point Tara thought she'd lost her phone. We were already demoralized, and this nearly broke us. She retraced her steps through the sagebrush while simultaneously patting every pocket she owned. The phone was eventually found in an obscure pocket, and we celebrated like we'd discovered fire. Our phones are our navigation, weather, communication, and sanity. Losing one would have been nearly catastrophic.

The mud was on a section of private land open to public use. Once we reached the county-maintained road, the surface became sandy instead of sticky. We expressed deep gratitude for highway crews, unsung heroes of the GDMBR.

We scraped mud, rode a few miles, then were hit by a storm and ducked under our emergency shelter. This happened three times. I found pushing the bike easier than the previous two days of riding, which says something about the previous two days. As a runner, I think my pushing muscles are stronger than my biking muscles.

A few miles later we missed a turn and rode a mile downhill off the route. This was particularly demoralizing. Have we not reached the low point of the day already? Ben (our navigation app) and Maggie (the magenta line we follow) were not aligned. Never a good sign. We slogged back uphill, and then the sky opened and dumped rain in biblical proportions.

At 2 p.m. we called it. Steamboat was not happening today.

At the junction we'd missed, after we had backtracked, we ran into two hunters, exchanged brief pleasantries in the rain, and turned onto the correct road. Less than a mile later we found a campsite and set up in the rain. Surprisingly, the sun came out immediately afterward.

We spent the afternoon drying gear and cleaning mud off the bikes. Later we rode four more miles round-trip to find water. Dinner and breakfast secured.

Tonight, we are tired, chilly, wet, muddy, grateful, and very ready for tomorrow to be less… adhesive.

> There were days on the Divide, particularly the early mornings, when the cold got into my bones and refused to leave. Not dramatic cold, not the kind that makes for a good story, but the slow, creeping kind that dulls your thinking and makes your hands clumsy. My brain shrank to walnut-size, focused only on the next small task: stay upright, keep moving, don't let the wind win. It wasn't fear so much as a narrowing of the world. Everything unnecessary fell away.
>
> I'd felt that narrowing once before, years earlier, on a bike trip in the Blue Ridge Mountains. Cold rain, dropping temperatures, miles still to go. At some point I stopped noticing the scenery, stopped caring about anything except getting myself to the waiting car and warmth. I wasn't capable of helping anyone else, not with directions, not with encouragement, not with anything. Hypothermia makes you self-centered in the most primal way. The world collapses to a single point: survive this minute, then the next.
>
> As I reflect on the Divide and those cold mornings, when I was stripped down to that same small, shivering version of myself, I think of Leigh on Ironman race morning in Tempe, not the triumphant finish, but the moment that nearly ended everything before it began.
>
> The morning water temperature was 60.1°F, cold enough that wetsuits became mandatory. One by one, swimmers emerged from the river and made their way up the red carpet

toward Transition 1. Some ran, some jogged, some staggered. Even in wetsuits, many were visibly shaking.

Then we saw Leigh, after more than ninety minutes in that cold, cold water.

A medical support volunteer was holding her arm, guiding her slowly up the carpet. Her eyes were unfocused, her expression dazed. She stared at her feet as if willing them to move, squinting with the effort to stay upright. My heart stopped. I felt the blood drain from my face, mirroring her pallor.

We held giant cutouts of her two cats, our attempt at humor and encouragement, and she managed a faint smile before her focus dissolved into anguished tears. My own vision blurred. Her face was blotchy, both red and pale at once. The medical assistant eased her to the ground.

The wetsuit "strippers" struggled to peel the neoprene from her trembling body. She couldn't assist; the cold had rendered her helpless. Her lips were purple. A smear of dirt streaked her cheek and chin, as if she'd taken a dust bath like my chickens. I wondered if she had stumbled coming out of the water, if she'd hit her chin, if there were injuries we couldn't see. She wasn't speaking. We were held back by the fence, only a few feet away but utterly powerless.

We had expected to cheer her triumphantly out of the water. Instead, the scene dragged us back to the days after her brain surgery, the slow steps, the fragile balance, the uncertainty. I knew I wasn't the only one reliving those memories, though none of us dared say it aloud. At the same time, we were relieved she had made it out of the water at all.

Cold water strips heat from the body far faster than cold air. Even in a wetsuit, prolonged immersion in 60°F water can overwhelm the body's ability to stay warm. Leigh had been in the river for one hour and thirty-seven minutes, long enough for confusion, loss of coordination, and muscle weakness to set in. She later told us she had considered signaling for rescue but doubted she could hold onto the support boat. So, she kept swimming, stroke after stroke, until she reached land.

The medical support volunteer finally said, "I'm taking her to the warming tent." He guided her around the changing tent and out of sight.

Out on the Divide, shivering on the side of a mountain, I did what adventurers do, and kept moving, kept pushing forward until a warmth rebuilt in my core. Some people can push through those moments, to emerge on the other side of the helplessness, the fear, to find the stubbornness it takes to keep going when your body is begging you to stop. My cold was temporary. Hers had been dangerous. But the feeling, that razor thin line between functioning and failing, was familiar.

And like her, I kept moving. Not because it was heroic, not because stopping wasn't an option, because I wanted to. I could. I can. I will. I do. And I will continue, until I can't.

De-Mudding with a Newfoundland and Chickens

Day 38—Friday, September 23
39.6 miles today • 1,510.6 miles total
To Steamboat Springs

We woke up with the cows, literally. They wandered past our campsite, mooing their way toward a sunlit field across the road, looking far more rested than we felt. We had a steep mountain to climb, and the first four miles were uphill. After yesterday's mud debacle, we welcomed hills like old friends. Give us gravity over peanut butter mud any day.

The last 1.6 miles to the peak were a push, steep, gravelly, rocky, the kind of slope that turns determination into a full-body sport. It took us just under two hours to reach the summit. We reminded ourselves that we are choosing to do this. Yes, we are choosing to do this. It is a choice. Our choice. Keep pushing. We convinced ourselves that we would call it type II fun tomorrow.

The descent was chilly despite the sunshine; the temperatures having dropped after yesterday's storm. The backside of the mountain was also steep and rocky, so we crept down, stopping occasionally to adjust layers and inhale snacks.

Over approximately fifteen miles, we saw one truck, one motorbike, and one man on horseback with three dogs. The idea of driving a vehicle on these washed-out, rock-strewn roads is unthinkable to us. But apparently not to everyone. What we are doing is likely unthinkable to them.

By early afternoon we hit pavement and rolled into Clark. Population: one building. Inside that building: a deli. A miracle. As we pumped up our tires for the final 20 miles, I bent the core of my valve stem. Uh oh. I crossed my fingers and prayed the tire would hold air all the way to Steamboat Springs. Miraculously, it did.

Tara pulled us through a headwind for twenty miles. I tucked in behind her and worked hard just to stay in her wake. I marveled at her sustained strength as my fatigue felt demoralizing. A couple of gravel bumps up and down on the ride into town, but otherwise uneventful.

Steamboat Springs is full of athletes and cyclists. Tara joked that no one would notice us with our loaded bikes, but within minutes a middle-aged man pedaled up and asked if we'd talk with him and his friends about our trip. We always feel like what we are doing is normal, until someone reminds us it is maybe a bit crazy. And that we are NOT normal.

During lunch we scrolled frantically for lodging and somehow snagged an Airbnb room on a Friday night. Donna and Ed were lovely hosts. Donna and her daughter both work for United Airlines, and her daughter had even run United's services in Portland, Maine for a couple of years. I always enjoy a Maine connection.

After dropping gear, I immediately rode back into town to see if a bike shop could fix my valve stem. The mechanic was hesitant at first, but three minutes later I was rolling out the door. Bless that man.

We showered, ate Thai food, met Ollie the enormous Newfoundland, and were in bed embarrassingly early, in an upstairs room in their cozy home. Bliss.

Chapter 8: When the Trail Demands More

"We" are a "we" until you shoot a porcupine

We tell our stories in the language of "*we*." As a couple, that collective pronoun becomes a kind of shorthand, a shared identity, a shared history, a shared life. Until one day you are no longer a "*we*" and have to face the world as *me*. That shift can come through separation, death, or, in my case, when my husband abruptly moved to our cottage in Maine.

"There is nothing here for me," he said, sunk deep in depression. Yet I was there. What did that mean for *us*?

For years, "*we*" were the keepers of chickens, sometimes ducks, and the reluctant executioners of the weasels, coyotes, raccoons, and mink that slipped into our yard and stole our hens. I hated it, but we chose to reduce the mammalian population on our small acreage to protect our egg-laying girls.

"*We*" were a good shot with an old wooden-stock twenty-two rifle, John's family heirloom from a boyhood in the Maine woods in the 1930s. John's father, a WWII veteran, used it to shoot squirrels and tin cans off the rock wall. Passed down through the generations, it kept plinking cans and defending our small homestead. Without children, who would this fierce little tool defend next?

The summer John moved to Maine; he left our New Hampshire house behind. The house was no longer a home to him; New Hampshire no longer felt like home at all. He had recently lost his first girlfriend. She died of breast cancer at fifty-five, and he had accompanied her to a chemo treatment, holding her hand during the infusion. I was glad. Glad she had someone to hold her hand, while struggling with something truly hard. I was glad that someone was my kind husband. Grief rearranges a person. It rearranged him.

Yet, I felt abandoned, although emotional intimacy had always been a struggle for us. Fiercely independent, I didn't "need" him in the way he needed to feel needed. At that moment in his life, being needed was a kind of validation.

He told me they had talked about being young and couldn't remember why they broke up. He built a beautiful cabinet to donate to a fundraiser for her medical bills.

I lived alone for over a year, spending a lot of time with Roger and Annie. Roger, one of my two "boyfriends", had been slowed down with Parkinson's disease and was my designated "emotional support man." And I had a porcupine problem. It was killing the young trees that John and I had planted and nurtured for twenty years.

Still believing in the old "*we*" of defending our homestead, I decided to save the trees. Roger, unstable on his feet, not to mention with a gun, offered to come shoot it for me. That's what boyfriends are for. But with his instability, I couldn't call on him to do it, so I did it. I shot a porcupine. A small one. Out of a tree.

It took far too many shots. Each time, I cringed and prayed it would fall quickly. Each time, it looked down at me, accusation, fear, despair, disappointment, all in its eyes. I swear I heard it say "ouch". I am still tormented. It was awful. It was unforgivable. And it was the moment I understood that without the "*we*," I had no interest in carrying out the rituals of our old life.

Never again will I kill one of God's creatures. Live and let live. Although in our new home, John still defends our hens, I am fully cognizant that I am no longer a "*we*" in the acts of homesteading defense.

Fulfilling Zero Mile Day

Day 39—Saturday, September 24
0 miles today • 1,510 miles total
Zero Day in Steamboat Springs

We started the day by taking photos in front of wings painted on a brick wall, hoping they'd help us go faster. They did not.

We stayed with Donna and Ed again, and Ollie the Newfoundland supervised our morning. Donna extolled the perks of part-time airline work. I'm always on the lookout for a new career, but ideally one that doesn't involve working for anyone. But travel perks are a draw. A conundrum.

Ed made excellent coffee, and then Tara and I went to The Shack for a large breakfast. Did I mention large? There were no leftovers. Not even a crumb.

The rest of the day was a cleaning marathon. We scrubbed our bikes with toothbrushes, mud in every crack, cranny, and crevice, then had to buy new toothbrushes. We washed gear bags, dried everything in Donna and Ed's sunny backyard near their flock of chickens, and made phone calls. We bought a new notepad, butt cream, and other essentials. Dinner was Clyde's pizza, followed by a pint of ice cream that didn't stand a chance.

Bikes re-packed, bodies rested, spirits restored. A perfect zero day.

Riding the Eyebrow

Day 40 - Sunday, September 25
60.3 miles today • 1,570.4 miles total
To Radium

We left around 8 a.m. after saying goodbye to Donna, Ed, and Ollie. Their backyard hose and friendly chickens had been a gift. I have chickens at home and miss those girls and the morning feeding routine.

We started on the bike path out of Steamboat Springs, meandering along the Yampa River. Soon the houses thinned and we were back in ranch country—horses, cows, fences, fields, pickup trucks, magpies. We passed a pretty lake, then climbed to Stagecoach Reservoir and crossed the dam. A large sign warned of a mountain lion in the area. Excellent. Another species higher up on the food chain than us.

The reservoir was low from electricity generation and drought. We skirted it and began climbing again, eventually reaching Lynx Pass at over 9,000 feet. What goes up must come down. We passed an old stagecoach stop, then removed our shoes to ford a small, icy river. Then another climb, then a high ridge we called "the eyebrow", a level-ish contour line with a few bumps and spectacular views of the valley.

Tara's brakes were flat again, and we weren't sure there was any adjustment left. But then came the descent, one of the best on the entire Great Divide. Even with soft brakes, it was glorious. We dropped 2,500 feet to the Colorado River and the "town" of Radium, which consists of a boat launch, a few campsites, and pit toilets.

We arrived before six p.m., filtered water from the Colorado River, set up camp, and ate dinner. By the time we were cleaned up, it was past the Marsha Rule's 8 p.m. bedtime threshold.

The weather was spectacular, frost in the morning, then sunshine and temps in the 60s or 70s. Because we rode twenty miles beyond our plan, we mapped out a new schedule to meet up with Maggie, stay with Hollyanna in Breckenridge, and rendezvous with Larry and Mimi for three nights. The plan: 40+ miles each day for four days, then a rest day in Salida.

Colorado is already delivering.

Keep Your Gluteus Maximus Happy

Day 41 - Monday, September 26
48.6 miles today • 1,618.96 miles total
To Horseshoe Campground

Yesterday we added twenty bonus miles simply to avoid sleeping near 10,000 feet and freezing our bums off.

We woke in Radium to a heavy frost, a table full of magpies, and the memory of two freight trains that had blasted past our campsite like they were late for a very important meeting. The magpies had pecked holes in a couple of our cooking-gear bags, but at least they didn't steal anything edible. Western crows apparently believe in sampling, not shoplifting.

We rolled out around 8:30 a.m. and climbed toward Inspiration Point, spotting red-tailed hawks, horses, cattle, and log trucks auditioning for *Fast & Furious: Timber Edition*. One cyclist we passed announced, without hesitation, that his "perineum hurt." Three minutes of conversation and we knew more about his anatomy than his name. Tara, ever the nurse, offered ibuprofen. He declined, perhaps worried she'd escalate to a full pelvic exam.

In Kremmling we struck out on stove fuel but scored excellent coffees at Shooters Café. I attempted an ice cream but dropped it in the parking lot. Gravity remains undefeated and I fought off a flash of depression. We chatted with a woman who rode the first TransAmerica ride across the United States in 1976 and met Mandy, a young rider hauling a BOB trailer across the country. We picked up groceries and rearranged plans with Maggie, a friend from home, who was going to join us for a day of riding. We also updated our new friend, Hollyanna, on our plans to arrive at her home in Breckenridge the following night. Our friends must think we've lost our minds, but estimating mileage out here is like trying to predict the stock market during fluctuating tariffs.

Ten miles past Kremmling we reached the Williams Fork Reservoir and stopped for lunch. On the climb we narrated an entire imaginary book about the Great GM, gluteus maximus. Keep your GM happy, just as you would your general manager. One controls your career; the other controls your ability to sit. We had gone bonkers from the miles or the heat, we weren't sure which.

Before camp we passed a long "No Trespassing" fence topped with upside-down cowboy boots. In the adjacent field stood a tall, unmistakably phallic stone monolith, fenced off like a national treasure. We didn't dare approach; we didn't want to lose our biking shoes to the boot-eating fence.

We reached the closed Horseshoe Campground around 4:30 p.m. A pit toilet (no TP), a beautiful river for bathing, and aspens glowing gold in the late September light. Not certain why the campground was not officially open and too fatigued to ride further or change our plans again, we opted to stay. We cooked our best dinner yet—rice, beans, veggies—and ate in the last warm rays before the sun slipped behind the ridge.

A good day. A strange day. A very Great Divide Day.

Lots of Friends in One Day

Day 42 - Tuesday, September 27
46.2 miles today • 1,665.16 miles total
To Breckenridge

We camped near Ute Pass, and our friend Maggie met us at 8 a.m. to ride over the pass together. Five or six miles up, five or six miles down, and then she turned around and did it all again to get back to her car. That's friendship. That's also cardiovascular fitness I can only aspire to, riding the pass twice in one day!

Tara and I continued toward Silverthorne, Frisco, and eventually, Breckenridge. At REI we tried (and failed) to get Tara's brakes repaired, but after a couple phone calls, we found a shop in Breckenridge that agreed to take her in that afternoon, as soon as we could pedal there. We climbed the switchbacks up the massive Dillon Reservoir dam and then cruised the bike path into town, feeling like we were in a tourism commercial for the region. We passed lots of active people, Colorado was consistently living up to its' reputation.

Our evening stop was the home of Hollyanna Bates, whom I'd met just a week before leaving home. She was the race director of the Southport "Don't Rock the Boat" 5K, where the prizes were freshly baked pies. She mentioned she hosted riders via *WarmShowers,* an app used by cyclists to find friendly folks willing to take people into their homes for a night. And now here we were, Tara and I arriving like two dusty raccoons who'd wandered into a mountain chalet.

Hollyanna, her husband Woody, and their dog Sugar welcomed four of us, Tara, me, Larry, and Mimi. Larry and Mimi had flown to Colorado to reconnect with us. Mimi was healing from her crash and seeing her felt like a special gift. Hollyanna and Woody made carnitas and lemon mousse that should be on a Michelin menu. We slept deeply in their beautiful home near 10,000 feet. I continue to be grateful for high altitude medication.

Larry and Mimi would meet us again in Hartsel the next night, as Tara and I would ride there. After many comedic texts, emails and phone calls, Tara had secured a cabin for the four of us, far preferable to pitching a tent behind the local bar. And I was thrilled they'd be carrying some of my gear. I am not a purist. I am a realist with tired quads.

Reunited and It Feels So Good

Day 43 - Wednesday, September 28
48.3 miles today • 1,713.46 miles total
To Hartsel

We started with sausages and eggs, thanks to Hollyanna and Woody, and packed lighter thanks to Larry and Mimi. We ditched one tent, not for weight but for warmth. At this point in the trip, warmth outranks pride, and with similar odors, we were not offending each other.

We climbed Boreas Pass, which Tara declared "not boring at all." The grade was gentle thanks to the old railroad bed, and at 11,482 feet I reached the top without puking. Diamox: miracle drug. Side effects: tolerable. No puking: priceless.

Aspens glowed yellow. Dark clouds circled but never caught us. In the afternoon we passed a pair of talkative burros who seemed to be gossiping about us. We eventually reached the ranch lodge in Hartsel. It was mid-renovation, not yet open, but they rented us two rooms anyway. Tara had spent days tracking down the new owners and convincing them that our injured, and recently surgically repaired friend Mimi, could not be subjected to a tent, or sleeping behind a bar. The people were wonderful; the sleep was decadent.

Larry and Mimi arrived with Thai food, and we sat in the lounge, amid the animal heads staring down at us from the walls. After dinner and showers, Larry cut Tara's hair: long, red, heavy and hot. Tara then cut mine: short, thinner and dirty brown, now flecked with gray. We cleaned up our mess along with some of the construction debris and returned to the couches. We lounged in the great room, again, like two feral houseguests who'd been temporarily civilized, in the company of the sophisticated and the coiffed.

Arrival in Salida

Day 44 - Thursday, September 29
51.44 miles today • 1,764.9 miles total
To Salida

Sunrise at the Hartsel Lodge was pink and soft, illuminating cow hides on the floor and the numerous taxidermy trophies on the walls. Breakfast among the heads. Nothing like being watched by a dozen glass-eyed ungulates while eating oatmeal.

Mimi and I slept together, and it was wonderful to catch up. She is healing and in good spirits. We are so happy she was able to visit with us, and she and Larry are planning to return again in a few weeks to meet us at the finish.

Tara and I rode away from the lodge around 8 a.m. and aimed to meet Larry and Mimi mid-afternoon in Salida. We passed a fenced field of buffalo, including a baby, and endured miles of washboard roads, sometimes sitting, sometimes standing, sometimes stopping to give our wrists and undercarriages a break. The washboard road took a toll on both ends of the anatomy today.

With Larry and Mimi here, this was our final chance to bail out of this adventure. Now or never? We never questioned our decision at this stage. We were strong, committed to going the full distance and having fun.

Near Cameron Mountain we reached the high point of the day, then descended fast toward the Collegiate Range: Princeton, Harvard, Yale, Columbia, four 14,000-foot peaks lined up like an Ivy League admissions brochure.

In Salida we met up with Larry and Mimi at the Brown Dog Café for ice cream. And, joy of joys, we also reunited with Jon and Lois. It's always fascinating to compare our diverging paths, different campsites, different weather, different stories. Same exhaustion and exhilaration.

On Hollyanna's recommendation we ordered pizza, salads, and calzones from Amica, then met Jon and Lois for a beer at the brewery. Tomorrow would be a full rest day. A day dedicated to eating. A day where my only athletic goal was chewing.

Rest Day: A Masterclass in Eating

Day 45 - Friday, September 30
0 miles today • 1,764.9 miles total
Rest Day in Salida

Salida is unpretentious, artistic, and surrounded by mountains. Tara is ready to move here. How many babies do they deliver in the local hospital annually? A key attribute needed to confirm her desire to relocate here. The weather was perfect.

I began the day with coffee in the hotel room and maybe a cookie or two. At breakfast I sampled the automatic pancake machine (one button, two pancakes, witchcraft). Then coffee, OJ, cinnamon-raisin toast with butter, jam, and cream cheese, scrambled eggs, yogurt.

After breakfast we found a pastry shop. Mimi and I split a cinnamon roll and drank spiced sweet chai. Then grocery shopping, during which I opened the chips on the walk back. Back in the room I grazed: half a carton of peanut butter and chocolate Oreos, a banana, peanuts, raisins, Gatorade, and the rest of last night's calzone.

We repacked the bikes, wandered town, and I had a pre-dinner ice cream. Then Mexican food. Then another ice cream. I ended the night with sparkling water and brushed my teeth, hoping I'd be adequately fueled for tomorrow, and praying I wouldn't need a midnight snack.

Now that we have gratefully reunited with Jon and Lois, we planned to ride together for the next three or four days toward Del Norte. A couple of high passes ahead, some questionable weather, and the hope of reaching New Mexico before the snow flies.

Larry and Mimi departed back to New England with the promise to pick us up at the finish.

We spend a lot of energy pulling our pants up

Day 46 - Saturday, October 1
41 miles today • 1805.9 miles total
To Tomichi Creek Cabin in Sargent

Reunions on a long ride feel a bit like spotting wildlife: you never know when they'll appear, and when they do, you're instantly happier. This morning, right at 8 a.m., Lois and Jon materialized in the hotel lobby, punctual, cheerful, and layered like onions. We hadn't ridden together in days and seeing them again felt like the trail had snapped back into its proper shape.

Yesterday we'd also seen Mo and Harry, the two young rockets who pulled us through the Great Basin. Unfortunately, Mo had contracted giardia, proof that even the fast and fearless are still human, and likely the carcass contaminated water was the cause. They'd taken a couple days off so she could start medication. We weren't sure if they'd set off again today or were still curled up somewhere in town, recovering. Trail friendships are like that: you care deeply about people whose last names you don't know and whose futures you can't predict.

The morning was cold enough to make us grateful for every layer we owned, but not quite cold enough for toe warmers. Who have I become, not using available toe warmers? The forecast promised afternoon showers, so we aimed for the town of Sargents, with the determination of people who have absolutely no interest in pitching a tent in the rain.

Marshall Pass tops out at 10,842 feet. I'm still taking altitude medication, and I'm convinced it's the only reason I'm not lying in a ditch somewhere, gasping like a landed trout. No nausea, no racing heart, just steady climbing and the occasional gasp of awe. The sky stayed mostly overcast, but when the sun broke through, the aspens lit up like they'd been plugged into an electrical outlet. Their leaves were so bright they seemed to glow from the inside, as if each tree had its own personality and at least half of them were extroverts.

Being a Saturday, the road was busy with four-wheelers and campers. We reached the top around 1 p.m., bundled up, and began the descent. It was cold. Jon and Lois had brand-new waterproof mitts from REI, and we were openly jealous. I was wearing doggie bags on my hands, which worked surprisingly well and fit my self-image as a total dork.

At the Tomichi Creek Trading Post, the sky began to mist. We asked about one of their tiny cabins with two sets of bunk beds, and the price wasn't much more than camping. The size of the cabin was about the same as our tents. Easy decision. We'll take the cabin. Tonight, the four of us are cozied up in a 10x10 cabin, two sets of bunks, one small heater, and zero personal space. If these cabins get any smaller, we'll all be sharing the same pillow.

Tara and I grabbed coffees while Jon and Lois celebrated with ice cream cones. I had the bar add a splash of Bailey's to mine, and after a hot shower I felt like a new person. I was clean, warm, and profoundly grateful for walls. The rain tapped on the roof, and for once we didn't have to pretend we were "cozy" in a damp tent with the sound of precipitation hitting nylon.

An older couple from New Zealand, who passed us on the road today, are staying in the next cabin. And yes, that was an accurate statement, the OLDER couple, who PASSED us.

Jon and Lois both looked great. Their pants still slipped down now and then, but they were eating constantly, and Lois in particular seemed to have hollow legs. Spirits were high, and we were grateful to be reunited.

The Sucker Hole Day

Day 47 - Sunday, October 2
38 miles today • 1844 miles total.
To Gunnison, Colorado.

It was John's birthday, and I missed it, again. While he was warm, dry, and comfortably far from the mess we found ourselves in, we were busy being thwarted by mud, weather, and our own misplaced optimism.

It rained hard overnight, and we were grateful for the tiny cabin that kept us from floating away. Morning brought drizzle, but we ate breakfast, packed the bikes, and pretended the day was going to cooperate. The New Zealand couple next door, both in their seventies, both wiser than we are, announced they were staying put. They'd seen this weather before. We, on the other hand, saw a brief ray of sunshine around 8:30 a.m. and immediately fell for it.

Anyone who spends time outdoors knows what a "sucker hole" is: that little patch of blue sky that convinces you the weather is turning, even though every cloud around it is plotting your downfall. We marched straight into it like four people who had learned absolutely nothing from the last month.

The sun lit up the fresh white snow on the 14,000-foot peak to the west, and for a moment we felt chosen. Then we rode to the post office, mailed postcards, and headed out for thirteen uneventful miles of pavement. Spirits were high. Morale was good. The sucker hole was working.

Then we turned onto dirt.

Two or three miles later, we met Tara's least favorite surface: mud. Not just mud, **peanut butter mud**, the kind that ruins your will to live. A young man in a truck had warned us earlier to take the lower road to avoid the mud on the upper route. We listened. We were prudent. We were proud of ourselves. We took the lower road.

And then we hit mud anyway.

Tara took one look and yelled, "TURN BACK! GO BACK!" with the urgency of someone who has seen things. Jon, who had not yet experienced the horror, thought she was being dramatic. Then his wheels stopped turning and he became a stationary exhibit titled *Man in Mud.* Lois, brilliant as ever, had already steered into the sagebrush and avoided the worst of it. The rest of us were not so clever. Scraping MUD. Tara and I had experience with this.

We pulled out the maps, backtracked, and detoured toward Gunnison. It rained. We put our heads down and rode because the alternative was standing still in the rain, which seemed worse. No sense deploying the emergency shelter, the forecast promised rain all day, and the forecast was right.

We rolled into Gunnison and took refuge in the McDonald's parking lot, scrolling for accommodations like four wet raccoons looking for a place to dry out. Tent? No. Cabin? Maybe. Cheap hotel? Possibly. Then Jon found a Warm Showers host willing to take four people. Four. On short notice. In the rain. He told us to bring wine because his wife would not be expecting guests, certainly not four muddy cyclists who looked like we'd been dragged behind our bikes instead of riding them.

Our hosts were Jarrall and his wife, whose name escapes me, both chemistry professors at the local university, both cyclists, both far too kind for their own good. They have a daughter in college and a teenage son at home who stared at us like we were a wildlife documentary happening in his living room. Jarrall has raced the Divide in twenty-one days, which is a number we don't even say out loud. We've already doubled it and expect to triple it, and we're fine with that.

We washed our bikes in their driveway, mud sloughing off in thick rivulets. We filled our tires with Stan's. We hung wet gear everywhere. We used their kitchen like we'd been invited. And instead of sleeping in the garage, they insisted we sleep in the house once they saw the state of us.

A neighbor brought over warm apple dessert made with fresh apples. It was delicious, but it also reminded me that I'm missing Maine's apple season. Picking apples and eating cider donuts with

John is one of our annual rituals. Today's apple crisp was a little taste of home, and a reminder of how far from home we've wandered.

The forecast looks better tomorrow. We'll stay on pavement, aim for 60 miles, and try to rejoin the route. Our goal is a forest service campsite, assuming the weather cooperates. We're hoping the truly bad weather holds off until New Mexico, where at least we'll be cold at lower elevations.

Larry and Mimi are back in Boston and working on plans to pick us up in Antelope Wells. We're hoping to fly home around October 28.

Best laid plans, of course.

But if today proved anything, it's that we are stubborn, we are resourceful, and we will absolutely fall for a sucker hole every single time.

Chapter 9: Choosing Kindness Over Winning

Choose one: Your friend or winning

The question posed in my MBA law class was simple, yet it acted as a surgical strike on my worldview: *In a high-stakes competition, do you choose the most skilled partner, or do you choose your friend?*

I didn't hesitate. I was one of seven students, and as the debate unfolded, I realized I was a solitary island. I chose skill. I chose the ringer. I chose the person who would guarantee the win, because what was the point of showing up if not to reach the summit? I had spent my life operating under the "unreasonable expectation that people be reasonable", which was just a code for expecting everyone to be as obsessed with optimization as I was.

For two hours, I defended my position. I was baffled by my classmates. To me, they seemed sentimental; to them, I must have seemed like a machine.

It took years of "striving" to realize that my classmates weren't failing the logic test, they were passing a much deeper one. I had been so focused on the finish line that I'd forgotten to look at who was running beside me. I viewed life as a series of peak achievements, keeping my emotions tucked away like a pressed suit, reserved only for special occasions.

But maturity has a way of blurring the sharp lines of a balance sheet. As I've aged, the "skilled companions" have faded into the background, replaced by the sisters who tell me I'm being "just like Dad" when I get too rigid. They are the ones who don't care about my ROI but will happily roast me over a photo of myself looking absolutely wrecked after ten days in Thailand, wrung out, exhausted, and finally, human.

I used to think that winning was the only way to avoid being "less than." Now, I see that the highest achievement isn't the trophy; it's the camaraderie. It's the razzing, the shared history, and the loyalty of people who have seen you at your worst and decided to stay for the after-party.

Perhaps I cherish the close friends I have now because friendship was hard to cultivate when I was "the boss." I was promoted young, first to Technical Department Manager, then into roles with more people and heavier consequences. I took that responsibility seriously. Hiring, firing, and making decisions that shaped other people's lives didn't leave much room for easy camaraderie. I lost friendships along the way, sometimes because I chose fairness over favoritism, sometimes because I believed someone wouldn't thrive in the environment. Even now, I'm not always sure I made the right calls.

If I had to walk back into that classroom today, I'd take the seat at the back, look at the professor, and choose my friends. I would gladly lose the competition, if I got to keep the people.

Meeting the Local Sheriff on the way to Nowhere

Day 48 - Monday, October 3
64.6 miles today • 1908.5 miles total
Note: All but 9 miles today were ridden on pavement
To The middle of Nowhere

There's a particular kind of joy in being in the middle of nowhere, the kind that comes from knowing you can take care of yourself in an environment that frankly doesn't care whether you make it or not. My family and friends always ask the same questions: *What do you eat? How do you stay warm? Aren't you afraid?* The truth is days like this are the answer. You eat whatever you can carry, you stay warm however you can manage, and fear doesn't get much traction when you're too busy pedaling.

We said goodbye to our Warm Showers hosts in Gunnison, still amazed they let four muddy strangers sleep in their house, and rode the eight miles back the way we'd come. Then we turned onto paved Route #114, which felt like the trail finally cutting us a break. Smooth, predictable, blissfully mud free. We cruised up the canyon, enjoying the pavement and the quiet.

Lois was disappointed that Jarrall had promised big-horn sheep, moose, and elk, and we saw none of the above. Not even a stray hoofprint. But we did see a herd of pronghorn, and we saw them in the most dramatic way possible, just before the sheriff stopped us.

We had just crested North Cochetopa Pass, 10,135 feet, and were flying downhill, our bikes heavy with wet gear but rolling beautifully. Then an unmarked blazer pulled across the road, angled toward us, and stopped. A very large, uniformed sheriff jumped out. He moved with purpose. Not the "I'm here to help" kind of purpose. More the "I need to speak with you immediately about your speed on the downhill" kind.

Uh oh.

We slowed. We watched him. We all wondered what law we had broken. Speeding? Unlikely. Failure to stop at a sign? Possibly. Existing suspiciously? Always. Maybe he was after Lois and Jon for that trespassing shortcut a few days ago, the one that ended with a caretaker yelling at them, Tara and I grateful we took an alternative route.

He opened the back of his vehicle and rummaged through gear like he was preparing to intercept us. We braked harder. We exchanged looks. Jon and Lois were wary of law enforcement. I, on the other hand, grew up believing police officers were the people you went to for help. I had uncles who were a state policeman, a sheriff, and a New York City "cop," as he called himself. Granted, the NYC uncle used to flick open a switchblade in front of us kids for fun, but I still thought he was a good guy.

So, were we in trouble? Had we done something wrong? The list of possibilities was long.

But no. He just wanted to offer us Gatorade.

Orange Gatorade. Full calories. None of that diet nonsense.

We accepted immediately, dutifully following Jon's rule to accept all offerings of food and drink, no questions asked. We stood there drinking our Gatorade while the sheriff told us how quiet his patrol was. He must have been having a very slow day. We thanked him and continued on, refreshed and relieved.

We turned back onto the trail with about nine miles to go. The climb was steady but manageable, the dirt road solid, the sky overcast and chilly. As we crossed a meadow near the campsite, the sun made a brief appearance, just enough to remind us it still existed.

We stopped at site #6 of an "informal" campground, which is code for "a place where no one will bother you because no one else wants to be there." We were on the edge of a forest, looking out at a field and a snow-dusted mountain.

For the first time on the trip, we built a fire. The wood was wet, so it took all four of us contributing to Jon's efforts—blowing, rearranging, coaxing, and occasionally swearing. Tara inadvertently burned her socks in the resulting small blaze, which felt like an acceptable sacrifice to the gods of warmth.

Dinner was simple. The fire was imperfect. The temperature dropped fast. But we were warm enough, fed enough, and far enough from anything resembling civilization that the whole day felt like a win.

I've always felt most at home in the middle of nowhere. Maybe it's because I grew up in rural Maine, where solitude wasn't something you sought out, it was simply the default setting. Here on the trail, you learn early that comfort comes from competence: knowing how to stay warm, how to feed yourself, how to read the sky and the land and your own limits. Cities make me feel like I am on the wrong frequency; the wilderness makes me feel capable. There's a quiet satisfaction in being self-sufficient in a place that doesn't care whether you're there or not. Some people need crowds or noise or convenience to feel anchored. I just need a patch of forest, fresh air, and the knowledge that if something goes sideways, I can figure it out. Nowhere has always felt like home because nowhere is where I know exactly who I am.

This is what I love: the middle of nowhere, the satisfaction of self-sufficiency, and the quiet pride of knowing we can handle whatever the Divide throws at us, even sheriffs with Gatorade.

Two Days from New Mexico

Day 49 - Tuesday, October 4
44.7 miles today • 1953.2 miles total
To Del Norte, Colorado

We should be in New Mexico in two days. That thought alone was enough to get us moving this morning. We woke to sunlight hitting the mountain across from our campsite, the peak dusted in fresh snow. The weather is shifting, rain turning to snow at higher elevations, and every morning feels a little more like we're racing the season south.

We didn't set alarms, but we were awake with the light, which comes later each day as we drop in latitude. Our tents were wet when we first stirred, but as the sun rose and warmed the upper air, the cold air sank and everything froze solid. Nothing like a little morning physics lesson to start the day: wet → frost → stiff as a board.

The first two and a half miles were straight up Cameron Pass, and we hit the high point of the day before 9 a.m. It was not the only climb of the day, just the tallest one, which somehow feels like winning the prize before the race is over, with more competitive hills still looming. We did a happy dance at the top anyway. Another pass summitted. Where is Mimi with her cowbell when we need her? We think of her often.

The eighteen-mile downhill was glorious. Partway along it, we caught up to the New Zealand couple we'd met in Sargent. They're in their seventies, wise, cheerful, and apparently aging in reverse. They had taken the weather-smart option and stayed put while we rode to Gunnison, and yet here we all were, arriving at the same place a day later. I look forward to being seventy, more experienced, more patient, and apparently faster. They rested; we rode; they still beat us. Jon had said there was no benefit to riding that day, and he was right. We should probably listen to him more often, but don't tell him that.

We stopped for lunch partway up the next climb. Before setting off again, we layered on rain gear because the sky ahead was a wall of storm clouds. It was definitely raining somewhere in our future. A bit later, we stopped and took the rain gear off because we were too hot. Then we put it back on. Then we took it off again. The balance between overheating from exertion and freezing from evaporative cooling is a delicate, ridiculous dance. Hot, hungry, cold, hungry, hot, hungry, cold. The hunger is consistent. Our bodies are fickle; the weather is worse.

Eventually we turned down a dirt track with a fast, fun mountain-bike style descent. We were having such a good time dodging puddles we missed a right turn that circled around a moderate peak. We had to climb back up, but none of us minded. The downhill had been worth it, and the climb back was manageable. We passed rock formations, including one called Elephant Rock, and threaded through a narrow notch before dropping down to circumnavigate the airport. Signs for the Great Divide Route pointed us around the perimeter, clearly intended to keep people from cutting across the airfield. The shortcut was tempting, especially after adding a couple of extra miles, but we behaved.

We dodged every storm this afternoon and rolled into Del Norte dry: we had suffered enough with the wet and now the gods were smiling on us. First, we checked out the free camping in the town park. It had a depressed, deserted vibe, and the bathroom was barely functional, a "3" on our bathroom scale. We decided to upgrade to the nearby campground which had showers, laundry, and a covered pavilion, luxury compared to the free town park.

Jon and Lois headed straight to the campground, while Tara and I rode another half mile into town for coffee at a pleasant bakery. I won't mention the pastries. (Lois, you missed out.) I needed the caffeine, calories, and warmth to face the mountain of chores waiting for us once we arrived at our destination for the day.

We stopped at a tiny grocery store before heading to the campground. We arrived in camp just as a thunderstorm skirted around us. We set up the tent and cooked under the pavilion. Tara and I had fresh spinach with scrambled eggs, salsa, and cheese. We boiled extra eggs for lunches, copying Jon and Lois's system. We sorted food, repackaged everything, and shed as much weight and trash as possible. It rained and blew sideways, and we were grateful for the pavilion roof over our heads.

As we returned to our tent, our neighbors, an Alabama father and son here to fly fish, offered us s'mores. We accepted, naturally. Don't tell Jon and Lois; they were off showering and missed out. They hate missing calories and are wasting away, mere shadows of their former selves.

Tomorrow is our biggest climb yet: over 4,000 feet in one push. Indiana Pass tops out above 11,000 feet, and it's about twenty-four miles into the day. We're carrying five days of food, the most so far, and plenty of water. Service will be spotty, if it exists at all. New Mexico is going to bring new challenges: remote, dry, empty, and exactly the kind of nowhere that feels like home.

Lois

Lois sees the world in black and white, and there's something refreshing about that. She's an accountant by training and by temperament: practical, precise, and unbothered by the gray areas the rest of us get tangled in. If something needs fixing, she fixes it. If you're cold and wet on an adventure, her response is simple: *What did you expect?* There's no drama in her delivery, just a matter-of-fact acceptance that the world is what it is, and you deal with it.

She pushes herself harder than she'll ever admit, and she does it without a hint of bravado. No bragging, no theatrics, no need to be seen as strong, she just *is*. I learned a three-stage, clothing de-smell protocol from her, complete with steps A, B, and C, delivered with the precision of someone who has tested the method enough times to know it works. That's Lois: thorough, specific, reliable.

She never has a Type III adventure because she refuses to let things spiral that far. She's capable, strong, and relentlessly positive, even when life gives her every reason not to be. She chose life over convention long before cancer forced the question, and then she chose life again when cancer tried to take it away.

One of my clearest images of her is on the side of a road, standing next to Jon, casually peeing with the help of her ostomy hose, holding it like a makeshift penis and announcing, "This is the best thing that came from having cancer." That is Lois in a single frame: unfiltered, hilarious, utterly unashamed, and somehow finding the bright edge in a place most people would only see loss.

She's understated but unforgettable. A person who doesn't need to shine to be luminous.

Jonathan

Jon is the kind of person you trust without having to think about it. He's real in a way that's rare: human, steady, occasionally frustrated, but never performative. Tough enough to race multi-day bike events, yet soft enough to light up when he talks about his dog, Winnie. There's a gentleness under the grit, the kind that comes from knowing exactly who you are and not needing to prove it.

If you asked who was the daring one in his marriage, I'm not sure Jon would claim the title. His wife might be the bolder spirit, the one who leaps first, but Jon is the quiet ballast that makes their leaps possible. He's the one who watches out for both, not out of fear, but out of care. There's a difference, and he knows it.

They've lived a life most people only sketch in the margins of their daydreams. They left traditional work young and moved to Chamonix, France, trading office walls for mountains and becoming snowboard instructors. Jon builds custom snowboards with the kind of craftsmanship that comes from loving the work itself. Later he found his way into a bike shop, the natural habitat for someone who lives by motion and mechanics. Every choice he's made bends toward passion, not convention.

Eventually they left the United Kingdom and resettled in a rural Canadian mountain town, a place that felt like it had been waiting for them. They travel often, not to escape their life but to expand it. They've dared to live exactly the way they want, and they've done it together.

Jon isn't untouched by Lois's cancer. None of us are. But he carries it quietly, the way he carries everything: with calm, with presence, with that wild, unbothered hair that seems to say he's long past worrying about what anyone thinks. He was willing to spend a year on a bike, and just as willing to turn back when health and sanity required it. That's Jon, courage in both directions.

He's the kind of steady that doesn't announce itself. You just feel it, like a hand on your back, keeping you upright without ever pushing.

Together

Jon and Lois together are a study in how two very different temperaments can create one beautifully aligned life. They move through the world with a shared purpose—quiet, steady, deeply intentional. This year they hope to ride across Kyrgyzstan in the Silk Road Mountain Race, the kind of undertaking that demands grit, humor, and partnership in equal measure. It suits them.

They're already custom outfitting a camper van so they can travel more freely, with Winnie as their third musketeer. Most days you'll find them in the mountains anyway—skiing, snowboarding, bikepacking, living the life they chose long before it was fashionable to choose anything other than traditional work. They've built a world around motion, mountains, and each other, and they carry that world with them wherever they go.

I now choose friends like these over winning every time.

Chapter 10: Discovering What Hard Really Means

What is Hard in Life?

Some days on the trail taught me that "hard" isn't a single thing. It shifts shape. It arrives in different weights. It doesn't always announce itself. And the kind of hard that shows up on a bike in the middle of nowhere is not the same kind that shows up in the rest of a life.

There's a kind of difficulty you sign up for with both hands. The kind that comes with maps and mileage charts and a start date circled on the calendar. It's physical, measurable, and most comforting of all, finite. You can point to it on a GPS track. You can feel it in your legs. You can name it: headwinds, washboard, altitude, cold mornings, a climb that looks impossible until it isn't.

This kind of hard is honest. It gives back what you put in. It teaches you that effort has a rhythm, and that your body will rise to meet it if you let it.

Then there's the other kind, the kind that doesn't care how strong you are or how many miles you've ridden. The kind that shows up in the middle of an ordinary Tuesday and rearranges your life without asking permission.

It's the weight of responsibility. The slow unraveling of a job that no longer fits. The phone call you never wanted. The hospital room. The grief you carry quietly because there's no finish line for it. This hard doesn't reward grit with a view. It asks for endurance of a different kind—emotional, private, and often invisible.

Some seasons of life look easy from the outside. You can be surrounded by comfort and still feel like you're walking uphill into the wind. You can be capable and still feel lost. You can be admired and still feel hollow. Not all difficulty leaves bruises. Not all strength looks like triumph.

What I learned, on the trail and off, is that both kinds of hard reshape you. The chosen hard builds capacity. The unchosen hard builds depth. One strengthens your legs; the other strengthens your understanding of yourself. And between the two is the person you're becoming, whether you notice it or not.

Maybe this is why I keep signing up for the kind of hard that comes with dirt and sweat and long days. Because the miles I choose make the miles I don't choose more bearable. Because movement steadies me. Because effort clears the fog. Because finishing something difficult, on purpose, reminds me that I can survive the things I never asked for.

Detours and Dogs

Day 50 - Wednesday, October 5
70.6 miles today • 2,023 miles total.
To Antonito

We awoke to drizzle after a night of unending rain. The high mountains around us had fresh snow, but most of the peaks were hidden behind low clouds, so we couldn't tell how deep the new snow was. We lingered under the pavilion, talking through the pros and cons of attempting Indiana Pass, the highest point on the entire route, versus creating a detour. We all wanted to go over the pass. It felt like a milestone we should reach, the crown jewel of the Divide. But the combination of new snow, rain in the forecast, and our collective desire not to die of hypothermia pushed us toward the prudent choice. On a future trip, the ride up Mount Lemmon, we would make the opposite decision and regret it, but today we erred on the side of survival.

We made breakfast under the pavilion, packed our damp bikes, and called the sheriff's department and local police, hoping for intel on road conditions. No luck. No one seemed to know anything about the snow depth up high, which did not inspire confidence. We rode into town for last-minute batteries, still debating our decision, but at least prepared with charged headlamps and navigation units.

All day we watched rain clouds circling us like a slow-moving carousel. Curtains of rain in every direction. Glimpses of snow on the mountains whenever the clouds lifted. And then came the irony: on the very day we didn't climb the highest pass on the route, the terrain was completely, utterly flat. Not rolling, not gently sloping, flat. We rode 70 miles, our longest day yet, and didn't go up or down. Just straight, flat roads, alternating between pavement and dirt, with ninety-degree turns like we were riding on graph paper. Did I mention there were no hills? It was strange, a little disappointing, and oddly enjoyable.

We passed cattle farms, endless hay and straw bales stacked to the sky, goats, sheep, cows, horses, and even an elk farm. And dogs, so many dogs. Fenced dogs, loose dogs, big dogs, tiny dogs, every color and breed. It felt like the unofficial "Dog Day" of the Great Divide. We also passed a few unfortunate critters on the road, mostly jackrabbits and porcupines, and tried not to look too closely.

When we reached the small settlement of Antonito, we ducked into the grocery store for bananas, bars, and Gatorade. We all pulled out our phones, hoping to find a place to stay in town, but nothing was available. So, we rode another five miles to the Twin Rivers Campground.

It started raining as we checked in, and we all became chilled. Fortunately, the campground had a communal building with a wood stove—warm, dry, and perfect. We set up our tents in the wet grass before parking our bikes inside the building. We then planned tomorrow's route, grateful to be sheltered for dinner and a planning session.

Today was our fiftieth day of riding and we rode seventy miles, our longest day yet. In that stretch I realized I felt strong, the days of riding manifesting into both leg and core strength. Not fresh, not invincible, just steady. Capable. The kind of strength that doesn't arrive on schedule, but shows up late, after you've stopped expecting it. Endurance has its own strange math: you can drag for days then suddenly find a gear you didn't know you still had. Or maybe it was just because the road was so flat!

> That late-trip steadiness reminds me of Leigh in Tempe, not the crisis, but the moment she reappeared on the course when we were hoping and praying that she could, though we weren't certain.
>
> After the medical tent swallowed her, we stood at the fence, frightened and helpless, watching months of training slip

through our fingers. It felt like witnessing a disaster unfold in slow motion. Then Brad's phone buzzed with an automated update from the Ironman app: "Athlete 1100 has entered the bike transition zone."

Great, we thought. If she just entered, we'd get over to the bike exit area in time to see her ride out. We rushed over and took our positions by the bike racks.

"Where is she?" Brad asked.

"Can you see her?" Angela added.

"We couldn't have missed her," I insisted, though my stomach was tightening. Athlete after athlete grabbed their bike and rode away. The racks emptied. Leigh did not appear.

I imagined her curled on the floor of the changing tent, still too cold to function. I felt sick. Surely something had happened. Surely, she had withdrawn.

I hurried back to the medical tent. The same young man was there, along with a young woman. I was shaking with adrenaline when I asked again about Leigh.

"She left medical quite a while ago," the woman said. "I helped her."

"We haven't seen her on the bike," I said. "Could you check the changing tent?"

"I helped her change," she repeated gently. "I'm quite sure she's gone."

I didn't believe her. Five of us had been watching intently. How could we have missed her? Had she fallen between the tent and her bike? I scanned the area, nothing.

"Maybe we missed her," I said, though doubt clung to every word.

"I can check if her bike is gone," the woman offered.

"Yes, please," I said. "Her husband and family are really worried."

She walked into the bike area, found the rack for athlete #1100, and returned.

"Her bike is gone," she said. "She's a sweet person. I helped dress her in the changing tent. We had warming packs on her. She was determined to keep going. I'm sure she's out on the course."

Finally, it sank in. Leigh was out there. She was riding.

We drove out onto the bike course to catch her on the loops. At mile twenty-seven, we finally saw her. She looked strong. We waved, cheered, and flashed the cat-head cutouts. I expected relief to wash over me, but the day was long, and my nerves were frayed. Spectating was unbearable. Competing was easier, I knew that stress. This helplessness was torture.

We saw her again on the second loop, smiling and eating a gel. Then again at the road crossing. Then twice more near the turnaround. By then, we were emotionally spent. We returned to the hotel, collapsed on the beds, and watched her progress on the app.

Later, we stationed ourselves near Transition 2 and cheered with relief as she rode in. She had finished the 112-mile bike ride. Stage 2 complete.

Out on the Divide, in the middle of that seventy-mile day, I imagine I felt like Leigh at this stage of the race. That late-trip steadiness is something I recognize more clearly now, after watching Leigh in Tempe, the way she had emerged from the cold, from the fog, from the place where quitting would have been the logical choice, the way strength sometimes returns late, quietly, without fanfare.

And sometimes, after hundreds of miles, you find yourself moving forward with a steadiness you didn't know you still had.

Tomorrow, we cross into New Mexico, where the mud is legendary and the services are scarce. But tonight, we have a roof, a stove, and the satisfaction of having made the right call, even if it meant trading the highest pass on the Divide for the flattest day of our lives.

Sunglasses MIA

Day 51 - Thursday, October 6
43 miles today • 2,066.8 miles total
To Chama

We woke up in our tents inside a building. A new level of Great Divide luxury, the kind of opulence only desperate, soggy cyclists can appreciate. After storing our bikes in the campground's community hall and cooking dinner beside a woodstove that radiated more *philosophical* warmth than physical heat, we simply couldn't face returning to the wet grass and damp nylon. So, we carried our tents, fully pitched, indoors like hermit crabs relocating to a larger shell. In the chaos, Tara's glasses became MIA.

This morning, Jon coaxed a small fire out of last night's ashes with monk-like patience, but the building was so cavernous the heat floated straight to the rafters and stayed there. Still, waking up dry felt decadent, like we'd checked into a five-star hotel that just happened to have concrete floors and a faint smell of mouse.

It was near freezing but sunny when we rolled out. Before leaving, we searched for Tara's sunglasses (still MIA) and replaced her missing shoe clip with one of our spares. Then we rode about seventeen miles before beginning the five-mile climb to the first pass. UP, naturally. The road twisted through vibrant aspens, and a narrow-gauge tourist train chugged by, apparently a pilgrimage site for train enthusiasts, who waved at us with the zeal of people who have never pedaled uphill at altitude. They showed no compassion.

We ate lunch on the first summit, Manga Pass. The second pass, Cumbres, topped out at 10,022 feet. The Cumbres & Toltec Railroad crossed the Colorado–New Mexico border multiple times, and with peak foliage underway, every lodging option within forty miles was booked by people who love trains more than we love riding.

We rolled into Chama (off route) and stopped at the Boxcar Café for Wi-Fi and a "snack." Jon and Lois ordered full breakfasts. Tara and I had soup, fries, and coffee. Just a light pre-dinner nibble.

Tara worked her magic and found us a room after calling eight fully booked places. Once we arrived, I had a sandwich (my second pre-dinner snack), cookies, and a handful of trail mix. Then we made dinner: spinach, broccoli, beans, rice, and cheese in tortillas. Jon and Lois returned from the store with a bag of chips, which exerted a gravitational pull on our hands every time we walked past.

Then came junior mints, cookies, and tea. A very balanced diet, if the food pyramid were shaped like a convenience store.

In the evening, we mapped out a two-day reroute to reach Abiquiu while avoiding MUD. Fingers crossed.

Expired Ding Dongs for Breakfast

Day 52 - Friday, October 7
59.9 miles today • 2,126.7 miles total
To Abiquiu

Breakfast at the hotel consisted of cold cereal, English muffins, and Ding Dongs that were only six months past their prime. Ding Dongs, for the uninitiated, are crème-filled chocolate cake coated in a waxy shell that tastes like nostalgia and regret. Jon ate one yesterday and survived, so I took my chances.

This daring culinary risk reminded me of a ten-year time capsule we buried in our yard one year. My brother Nick said he would cook and eat the dehydrated meal if it was still intact after ten years. Ten years later we dug it up and two items were fully intact, the Styrofoam paper plates with the stars and stripes, and the dehydrated meal. He did not die either.

We chose the road route from Chama to Abiquiu to avoid the dreaded mud. Today the scenery changed dramatically, with high mountains and aspens giving way to dry desert, red sandstone bluffs, and sky so wide it felt like someone had increased the aspect ratio of the world.

We took turns pulling at the front, breaking the wind for the others. The road rolled gently, and the wind was merciful, an unusual combination that made us suspicious, like nature was luring us into a trap.

We stopped at a wonderfully odd gas station and bar for ice cream. The walls were covered in $1 bills, presumably left by people who wanted to be remembered for their financial contributions to the arts. There was no space on any wall or the ceiling to add another bill. Then we continued to Echo Amphitheater for lunch. The natural amphitheater's carved canyon walls displayed thousands of years of sedimentation, nature's version of a layer cake, minus the frosting.

We passed Ghost Ranch on the final twelve miles into Abiquiu, the red cliffs rising in those familiar, impossible shapes that Georgia O'Keeffe made famous. Even if you don't know her work well, the landscape feels like it's been painted already, like you've pedaled straight into a canvas. Twenty-one thousand acres of mesas, desert sky, and geological drama, all carrying that strange mix of art, science, and spirituality that seems to cling to northern New Mexico. If Mimi had been with us, we would've stopped without question; she's an O'Keeffe devotee and would've marched us straight into the visitor center before we could unclip. My friend Peter knew it too, he'd spent time there years ago, doing one of the spiritual programs and learning carpentry skills in the process. Only a retreat like Ghost Ranch could combine enlightenment and power tools and make it feel perfectly natural.

We, however, were on a mission for coffee, ice cream, and groceries, and the access road to the ranch was miles long, so we rode right past it—and past our campground, Retreat on the River—into town, then doubled back with our spoils. The place was small and scrappy in a way that felt right for the day: a few buildings, a tent area, a communal kitchen, and an outdoor shower that was more functional than luxurious. The sauna was out of order, which was disappointing; we had envisioned a cleansing. But the deck overlooking the Rio Chama made up for everything. We ate dinner there, legs dangling over the edge, drinking tea like a pair of desert mystics who had absolutely earned the right to sit still and watch the river move.

Other campers were around, including hikers on the Continental Divide Trail. Tomorrow, we rejoin the GDMBR for what is rumored to be the steepest section yet. Two days to Cuba, our next resupply.

Cinnamon Buns and Tarantulas

Day 53 - Saturday, October 8
30.5 miles today • 2,157.2 miles total
To the Ridge Above Abiquiu

The guidebook warned us that today would be the most challenging day of the entire route. It was right. The whole day was uphill, rough, rocky, and the kind of slow grind that makes me wonder why gravity has a strong preference for me to stay closer to sea level.

We biked into Abiquiu first thing and stopped at the "store," which turned out to be a small structure held together by hope and cinnamon sugar. It had a cinnamon bun. A real one. Where are you Mimi, my co-lover of cinnamon buns! I had to eat it by myself, though it was not such a difficult chore. We also filled up with extra water because we were heading up onto a ridge with no water for almost 80 miles over two days. Nothing says "adventure" like rationing hydration.

Shortly up the trail we saw a tarantula. A big, black, hairy one, sporting a tan back like it had dressed up for the occasion. It was our only wildlife encounter of the day, and we gave it plenty of space.

The climb was gradual at first, and we stripped off layers as we rose into a desert landscape dotted with cacti, some fruiting with bright red orbs. We passed a massive, towering wall of columnar basalt, the kind of geological feature that makes you feel small and temporary. Hunters in trucks rumbled past occasionally, reminding us some people choose horsepower over leg power.

Eventually the rain arrived. We put on all our rain gear and kept climbing. Did I mention the whole day was up? Our plan was to go twenty-three miles, a modest goal given the difficulty, but we managed to push further.

> As I reflected on that endless climb, when rain was dripping off my helmet, mud collecting on pants, running down into my shoes, gravity insisting I belonged closer to sea level, I found myself thinking about what we consider "difficult" or what we call "hard." People will look at this trip and say it must have been the hardest thing I've ever done. But difficulty feels different when you choose it. When you sign up for the suffering, pack it neatly into panniers, and pedal straight toward it.
>
> I've spent my life gravitating toward curated difficulty: marathons, rock climbing, long days on SAR teams, the kind of challenges that demand focus and grit but come with an exit ramp. You can always stop running. You can always come off the wall. You can always say no to another mile.
>
> Out here, even on a day like this—wet, cold, uphill in every direction—the hardship is voluntary. I chose this. I wanted this. And that choice changes the weight of it. The Divide sharpens you, but it doesn't break you, because you walked into the difficulty with your eyes open.
>
> The truly difficult things in life have never been the ones I trained for. They've been the ones that arrived uninvited, without permission, and without a map. But today's climb? Today's grind? This is the kind of hard that reminds me I'm alive.

We passed a low area with flash-flood warning signs, which felt like an unnecessary threat given that we were already wet enough to have been swimming.

Earlier in the day we'd seen flocks of bright blue bluebirds, but by afternoon the world had narrowed to drizzle, mud, and the sound of our own breathing. When we reached the initial campsite, it was wet, unappealing, and too early to stop. So, we kept going, finishing the climb.

At the top we stopped to eat and put on dry clothes, as Tara's rain gear had soaked through despite two waterproofing treatments. We decided to start down, gaining miles on the plan for tomorrow, and to stop as soon as we found an attractive stealth-camping spot. Within a few miles, we found a level patch off the road, far enough from the trail to feel hidden. We'd only seen a handful of cars and four-wheelers all day.

The rain stopped long enough for us to set up the tent and cook dinner. We were inside by 7:30 p.m., studying maps for tomorrow. We're sleeping at 10,140 feet tonight. Again, I'm grateful for the Diamox; without it, I'm a guaranteed puker at 7,000 feet. The landscape on this side of the mountain has shifted again, no more desert cacti and sage, but high mountain aspens, Ponderosa pines, and cedars.

Someday I WILL eat a Grasshopper

Day 54 - Sunday, October 9
50.75 miles today • 2,207.95 miles total
To Cuba, New Mexico

When we got up this morning, we realized we had camped in a cow field above 10,000 feet, and early-morning hunters were already on the road as we packed up. The sun was out, but it was still freezing—one of those mornings where you put on layers for the downhill and strip them off for the uphill. The temperature swings between sun and shadow were dramatic enough to have us vacillating between shivering and perspiring.

I heard grasshoppers again and felt hopeful we were progressing back into warm weather. I was wrong, but hearing them reminded me of Montana and Wyoming, where grasshoppers were everywhere and we were hungry enough to consider roasting them in oil with a lot of salt. I imagined early settlers doing the same. When we saw a box of dried grasshoppers in a five-and-dime store in one of the small towns, I was tempted to buy them, but I didn't. If only they were fresh and not imported from China. Ya, right. Faced with fresh ones in Thailand, I still refused. I'm not sure why, as I still think of them as a possible food source.

With no wood for miles, just sagebrush, the cow patties made perfect sense as fuel. Humans are endlessly creative when faced with an abundance of the wrong thing.

The downhill was rough and rocky, fully testing the limits of a "gravel" bike loaded like a pack mule. Bump, bump, bang, thump. Eventually the terrain smoothed into dirt road with short sections of red muck that, thankfully, didn't stick to our tires.

The sky was mostly overcast, with occasional sun. At lunch, the sun came out long enough for us to dry our tents and jackets from yesterday's rain. We dug them out of our panniers and spread them in the sun. After lunch, we saw hail on the ground as we topped out on a high point and were grateful it hadn't hit us directly. A little while later we saw a blue sucker-hole in the sky, just before the big rain event. We got drenched.

At one point, the rain was so heavy we pulled into a pit toilet for shelter. Glamorous, I know. This was the first time we would save ourselves in a pit toilet, but on this occasion, we didn't have Mimi and therefore no gummy worms. Hunters were everywhere, also trying to avoid the weather—in trucks, on four-wheelers, and in campers tucked into the trees.

Standing in a pit toilet to escape a storm is the kind of discomfort I can laugh about later, because even on a day like that, the hardship was temporary and I chose to be here. But the cold and the rain made me think about the things in life we don't get to choose—the ones that don't end when the clouds lift.

> I've handled plenty of difficult situations, but the hardest ones were never physical. They were the moments that arrived without warning: telling a hundred employees we couldn't make payroll, standing in a manufacturing plant at one in the morning

while a piece of equipment burned, watching an employee spiral into addiction while still being one of my best workers. Those weren't endurance tests; they were reckonings. There was no finish line, no summit, no map.

And then there are the things that happen to the people we love. Roger with a Parkinson's diagnosis. John losing his hearing, the word *profound* landing heavier than any storm. Leigh's brain tumor—the kind of news that rearranges a family's internal architecture. Annie caring for a spouse with Parkinson's. Leigh beating cancer and then choosing to race a full Ironman—a different category of hard entirely.

Compared to that, riding into freezing rain feels almost simple. Miserable, yes. But simple. You keep pedaling, you get to town, you warm up. The unchosen hard things don't offer that kind of clarity.

Once back on the bikes, the rain continued. The last ten miles into Cuba were downhill on pavement, in cold rain. Before the descent, Tara put on her down jacket and we added toe warmers to her gloves. She was very cold from having stopped, and we were truly worried about her safety. Tara would have been better off to push through without stopping. Group dynamics don't always benefit the individual. My mittens were sopping wet but warm thanks to toe warmers. Toe warmers continue to be the unsung heroes of this trip.

We rolled straight into McDonald's to warm up and Google town amenities. My new fashion statement was wearing the toe warmers on my ears. I was glad we made it to town, but still quite worried about Tara recovering from that cold downhill. French fries and coffee never tasted so good. Jon rolled his fries into a wrap and introduced us to the British "chip butty," a French-fry sandwich. Who knew that was acceptable? We all did warm up.

We booked a room at the Frontier Motel for $80. Low expectations, but any place that lets us bring our bikes into a ground-floor room is appreciated. We walked to a Mexican restaurant for dinner. Everything we own is wet or damp. It will take a full day to clean and dry our gear, which is the plan for tomorrow. Happy to be sleeping in a bed.

In bed early.

An Easy Day in Cuba

Day 55 - Monday, October 10
0 miles today • 2207.95 miles total
A Day in Cuba, New Mexico

We needed a day to dry gear and wash clothes. We started at the gas station for coffee while Lois slept in. A man in line had a gun—large, visible, and intimidating. He was wearing jeans and a hoodie and turned out to be perfectly pleasant. Jon and Lois, coming from countries where guns aren't part of the morning coffee routine, are understandably unsettled when guns are so visible.

Back at the motel, we had breakfast in the room, then headed to the laundromat. I'm sure we were all naked under our rain pants and jackets while everything we owned spun in the machines. A couple of hikers came in and said their hotel room had bedbugs, and they had to launder everything. Misery loves company, and their misery was far worse than ours.

> Sitting in that laundromat in rain pants, watching everything we owned spin in the machines, didn't feel profound at the time—it was just another odd moment in a long string of odd moments on this trip. But looking back, I found myself thinking about how easy it is to misjudge what "hard" looks like from the outside.
>
> My life has been full of privilege: a reliable car, a house my husband built board by board, decades of outdoor adventures. And still, there were seasons when I felt lost or unsure of my place in the world. Hard doesn't always announce itself. Sometimes it's quiet, internal, invisible.
>
> What I've come to understand is that the difficulty we choose—running marathons, climbing rock faces, riding a bike for sixty-six days—builds strength and confidence. But the

difficulty that chooses us builds perspective. And maybe wisdom, if we're lucky.

The quiet gift of this trip is realizing how much I admire the people around me who face the uninvited kind of hard every day—friends, family, strangers—and how much I want to meet my own life with that same steadiness.

Jon rode to the ranger station for route information, but it was closed as it was Sunday. In the parking lot he met the man with the large gun again, named Dave, who said he'd come to our hotel in twenty minutes to review maps with us. Great idea: invite a stranger with a gun to our hotel room in Cuba, New Mexico. We opted to meet him outside.

Dave showed up. He reviewed the maps on the hood of his car and freely gave us advice about muddy roads and safety near the border. He said we might encounter people who had crossed illegally, but they were usually in need of water, not dangerous. He was kind, knowledgeable, and unexpectedly helpful. Eventually Lois asked him, "Why do you have a gun?" Turns out he was the chief of police in this small town. Formal uniforms were unnecessary.

Lois and Jon seem to attract law enforcement. Hmmm.

We shopped for food and spent the day cleaning bikes and repacking. Why does it take so long to repack so little stuff? Tara met her cousin for lunch, who brought gear from REI—waterproof mitten covers for both of us. Tara had also ordered other sought-after gear improvements: a better rain jacket and a sleeping mat with a higher R-factor. Who knew sleeping mats were rated for warmth like wall insulation? I grazed all day, trying not to eat all the Oreos.

Tomorrow we head toward Grants, two days away. Tomorrow night we'll sleep behind a gas station, behind a locked fence. That should be interesting. The next night our plan is to stay at a hostel in Grants.

Camping at a Gas Station

Day 56 - Tuesday, October 11
48.8 miles today • 2256.75 miles total
To Chaco Trade Center

It's only 3 p.m., but with no camping for the next seventy miles, we've resigned ourselves to spending the night beside an abandoned railroad car behind a gas station on Navajo Nation land. The owners allow camping, which is generous, though the setup feels a bit like we've been checked into a low-budget zoo exhibit. A very tall chain-link fence surrounds the lot, and it is locked at dark. The proprietors made sure we understood that part. Once the gate closes, we're in until morning. I'm half-expecting a school group to wander by and read a plaque about "The Endangered Long-Distance Cyclist in Her Natural Habitat."

This morning Tara mailed home her old rain gear. Grateful for her cousin's visit yesterday, we look forward to our new over-mitts and dispensing with the doggie bags for our hands. The trip to REI was fruitful and the new gear appreciated. We're now saving the doggie bags for our feet, if needed. It wouldn't be the first time we've wrapped our toes in plastic. On one of our early multi-day trips, from Pittsburgh to Washington, D.C., we rode two days in sweltering ninety-five-degree heat, followed by a third day of chilly rain. By late afternoon I was on the verge of hypothermia. We ducked into a deli, dried off in the restroom, ate something hot, and borrowed their sandwich wrap to layer over our fresh socks before shoving our feet back into wet shoes.

Today's miles were fast. Rolling hills, no major climbs or descents. The morning sky was a perfect blue, not a cloud in sight, and it was nearly 50°F when we left, warm by our recent standards. The landscape was scrubland and low sagebrush, a few cows scattered here and there. At one point four horses raced us along the fence line for a couple of miles. They genuinely seemed entertained by beating us. They'd sprint ahead, stop at the next fence break, wait for us to catch up, and then take off again. Nothing like being taunted by livestock to keep you humble.

By afternoon, white puffy clouds drifted in, beautiful, but also a reminder that rain would turn this gas-station, railroad-car, solar-array situation into a mud pit. We're hoping the sky holds. Mud is not on my list of preferred sleeping surfaces.

First order of business on arrival: ice cream. No need to rush, we're early and have nowhere else to go. The gas station locks the gate at 8 p.m. and opens it at 7 a.m. We're grateful for the water source, but it's going to be a long night. I don't even have a book. Just us, a railroad car, a solar array, and a chain-link fence. Living the dream.

Lois Levitates

Day 57 - Wednesday, October 12
72.1 miles today • 2328.85 miles total
To Grants

Seventy-two miles today, our longest yet, and it finally felt like New Mexico. Warmer air, no frost, no toe warmers. We lingered at the gas station with free coffee, waiting for the sun to crest the horizon and dry our tents. Blue sky, sagebrush, light wind, and one rattlesnake who sent Lois three feet straight up on her bike.

The whole day was on pavement, another steady climb followed by thirty miles of blessed flat and downhill. My legs are stronger now, but a long day on the seat is still a long day on the seat. We passed a massive mine and rode under a tunnel the company built to shuttle ore from one side of the road to the other. Then a long train in Milan held us up before we rolled into Grants on old Route 66.

Tonight, we're in our first hostel, which feels like a social experiment. Dinner was shish-kebab chicken, salad, and asparagus from the grocery store, grilled in the backyard. It tasted like a real meal. The hostel runs on solar, so when the power's gone, the lights go out.

The owner, who works for the forest service, reviewed the next stretch of trail with us, and he believes it is dry enough to ride, with a few detours around puddles. Tomorrow, we leave pavement again and head back to dirt. We expect to reach Pie Town in two days and Silver City four days after that. We are getting close to the finish.

Zzzzzz.

Back on the Trail, Best Day Yet!

Day 58 - Thursday, October 13
43.8 miles today • 2372.65 miles total
To Wild Camping before Pie Town

We woke up to practically naked Ranger Ross in the kitchen, his cats happily licking the butter left out on the counter. Then Ross cooked with it. Ick. Our first hostel experience was… educational. There were three or four Continental Divide hikers staying there too, and we had a room with double queen bunk beds. At this rate, we're getting closer to Jon and Lois every day. Soon we'll be four to a bed. Probably a good thing we're nearing the end of this journey.

The hostel *did* have a great bike stand and tool set, which was a great amenity. We had washed clothes and hung them out to dry the night before. I hung the tent out for a few minutes in the morning and it dried quickly. There was no solar power left early this morning, so no lights and no internet when we got up. Off-grid whether we wanted to be or not.

We left after breakfast and headed toward the grocery store. A cluster of towering metal Sasquatch statues stopped us in our tracks, and I wondered if the plural of Yeti was sasqui. Either way, we met a whole family of them. We laughed, took pictures, and matched their poses, because when mythical creatures invite you to play, you play.

The real work started afterward: shopping for six days of food, our longest stretch yet without resupply, and hauling two days' worth of water. When we finally rolled out, our bikes were the heaviest they'd ever been. They groaned. We groaned. Gravity sucks.

Packing food for bikepacking is like playing Tetris with calories. You suddenly realize how much useless packaging exists in the world. We strip everything down to the bare minimum, remove boxes, dump things into bags, squeeze out air, crush chips, flatten crackers. If it contains oxygen, we open it and squish it. Presentation is optional. On a later adventure, I survived a night on cracker powder alone.

While packing in the parking lot, Tara realized she was missing a bag of food. First the rolls were gone. Then the broccoli. Then the avocado. Then an apple. The previous customer must have absconded with an extra bag. The store kindly replaced everything, probably because they saw the desperation in our eyes.

Next stop: Walmart, for dehydrated food for Jon and Lois, bike lights for us, a lock, and shampoo. By the time we finally got back on the route, we'd already traveled nine miles before the day even started.

We climbed fourteen miles up through a canyon on a dusty road, trucks hauling firewood everywhere. People can collect firewood on national forest land with a permit and today seemed to be the day everyone decided to do it.

We stopped for lunch about ten miles before the summit. Tara suddenly said, "Hey guys, I lost one of my shoes!" She was clearly demoralized by the loss. We all turned to look at her, only to notice she was holding both shoes in her hands. We stared at her like she had three heads. Someone said, "Both shoes are in your hands." She was truly astonished. Are we losing it? Yes. Yes, we are. We take turns with the silly delirium.

The canyon was beautiful with red, horizontally striped mountains towering over us. We smelled a skunk at lunch and speculated it was a javelina—a collared peccary, apparently not in the pig family. We were wrong. (Definitely skunk.)

After the summit, we descended through lava fields, massive flows that looked like frozen rivers of rock. They stretched for miles, some much taller than others. I would've loved more time to explore; it's a geological wonder. There are also lava tubes a few miles off route in this region, but none of us wanted to lose a day to another adventure. Even we have limits on the miles we are willing to add for sightseeing.

We have now been on the bikes for more than fifty days and I can feel the momentum shifting. Not easier, exactly, but more familiar. My body knew what to do. The miles didn't intimidate me the way they had earlier. Even the climbs felt less like battles and more like agreements: I'll keep moving if you keep rising at a reasonable angle. It was the kind of rhythm that only shows up after weeks of effort, when fatigue and strength learn to coexist.

> When I think back on that late-trip steadiness, I see the same quiet determination Leigh carried through the marathon course in Tempe, the part of the race where so many athletes unravel, and she somehow came alive.
>
> Her transition to the run was quick, just ten minutes. She came onto the run course looking fresh and happy. We looked like we'd been through a war. She had nearly five hours of running ahead, so we left the race area, rested in the hotel for a while, then grabbed a ramen bowl for her post-race recovery meal and returned to the finish area after dark. When we reached the finish line, we estimated Leigh had about forty-five minutes left.
>
> The sun had long since slipped behind the desert skyline, leaving the course lit only by streetlamps, glow sticks, and the occasional headlamp bobbing through the darkness. The air had cooled, but the energy near the finish line was electric—cowbells, cheers, music pulsing through speakers, volunteers shouting encouragement to the athletes pushing through the last brutal miles.
>
> My stomach churned with a mix of dread and awe. She had already survived the cold-water swim, clawed her way through the bike, and now she was out there in the dark, running on legs that had been working for nearly twelve hours. I kept scanning the path, searching for her familiar stride.
>
> The finish chute was a long, illuminated corridor lined with spectators leaning over the barricades, shouting names, clapping, ringing bells. Every few seconds, another exhausted

athlete appeared, shoulders slumped, feet dragging, face twisted in pain. Some cried. Some limped. Some looked hollowed out. Some were strong; the first-timer bell was being rung frequently.

Then, in the distance, I saw a small figure rounding the final bend.

At first, I wasn't sure it was her. The lights cast strange shadows, and the runners all looked like silhouettes. But then I saw the ponytail, the determined forward lean, the unmistakable familiar rhythm of her stride—steady, compact, efficient. Leigh.

She wasn't shuffling or staggering like so many others. She was running. Running!

As she came closer, the crowd noise swelled, as if they sensed something in her, some quiet force pulling her forward. Her face was flushed, her eyes focused, her jaw set with that familiar stubbornness that had carried her through surgery, rehab, and every mile of training.

She spotted us, our cat-head cutouts raised high, and her expression cracked into a smile. Not a big one, but a real one. A smile that said: I'm still here. I'm still moving. I'm finishing this.

She lifted her hand and rang the "first-time finisher" bell hanging beside the chute. The clang echoed above the crowd, sharp and triumphant. The volunteers cheered. Spectators clapped. And Leigh, our Leigh, kept running.

Her stride didn't falter. She didn't wobble. She didn't break down. She ran through the finish arch with her head high and her shoulders back, as if she had been born for this moment.

The announcer's voice boomed over the speakers:

"Leigh, YOU are an Ironman!"

I recalled those late trip miles on the Divide, when my own legs felt unexpectedly sure beneath me. The way she ran not with ease, but with conviction. The way she finished not because she felt good, but because she refused to stop.

And in my own quiet way, I understood that. Some miles are powered by strength. Others are powered by something deeper, but her journey and race seemed far more difficult than my adventure.

As our day continued, the road surface became hard with dried mud. The warning sign was intimidating, asserting if you got yourself stuck in the mud, NO ONE was coming to help! We trusted that the weather had dried things "enough", or that Tara's early warning signals would turn us around! It was bumpy but fun. We passed a "point of interest" on our Bike Navigator app, a log house, which was significantly less exciting than the lava flows.

Tara set the Guinness World Record today, for heaviest bike held vertically while simultaneously peeing. No photos, but Jon was impressed.

We wild-camped tonight. The animal of the day wasn't an animal at all but the homes of animals, giant ant hills everywhere. I am fascinated by nature. How can something so small make such a large house? We ate some of our heaviest food to lighten the bikes for tomorrow but conserved water since we don't know when we'll find more.

The day was sunny and warm, shorts and short sleeves! Tonight brought an adventure in scary night noises. Hard to describe, but they were intimidating. Maybe it's just that "wild camping" primes the imagination for "wild animals."

I felt great today, crediting last night's real meal, but Lois was tired by the end of the day. We all have good days and bad days. Tomorrow will be a great day, though, as Pie Town awaits!

Goat Heads and Pie Town

Day 59 - Friday, October 14
52.37 miles today • 2425.02 miles total
To the Pie Town RV park

Hunters drove past our tents before we were even up this morning. As they rolled by, we overheard one of them say, "Divide riders," and they kept going. Apparently, there's enough bicycle traffic on the Divide locals now identify us like a wildlife species. Ah yes, the migrating Divide Rider in its natural habitat, emerging from its nylon cocoon at dawn.

The adventure of the day: goat heads. The dreaded thorns. Just as we were ready to leave, Tara noticed several embedded in our tires. We'd been warned not to pull them out, apparently that's an invitation for instant deflation, so we nervously left them in trying to have confidence in our Stan's, the liquid goo in our tires designed exactly for this situation. We rode away full of anxiety, as if we were rolling across a minefield, which we were.

Then Tara's rack bolt came loose and needed a new screw. Jon got a flat and expertly plugged it, but it was the beginning of a frustrating day for him. We have now confirmed, with scientific certainty, that we do not like goat heads.

The landscape was a mix of rolling hardpack and strange beauty with mud lava, hardened like rock, stretching across the landscape. The moon hung low over the sagebrush, giving everything a slightly surreal glow. We passed a windmill water tower, and Lois bravely ran the gauntlet through sagebrush and goat heads to check it out, but we couldn't figure out how to access the tank structure to extract water from it. So, we kept riding, slightly thirstier and none the wiser.

Lunch was on the road. Later we stopped at TLC Ranch (completely unexpected to find a ranch with our team's name!) where they leave water out for riders and Continental Divide hikers, in cooler jugs. The TLC ranch for the TLC riders, and it felt right. We instantly thought of Mimi and took photos with the ranch sign to send to her. The ranchers had provided cold water, conspicuously left in a shed near the ranch gate. Actual cold water. It felt like a gift from the gods. A Continental Divide Through Hiker was resting in the shade there, looking absolutely beat. We've all been that person at some point on this trip.

Pie Town was everything we hoped for and more. The Does and Buicks restaurant delivered miracles.

Miracle #1: We all ate pie.
Miracle #2: We all ate dinner.

Miracle #3: A friendly couple, Diane and Jim from Kansas, paid for everything. He raced the Divide in 2018, and now they're road-tripping in their van. Their karma is excellent.

Miracle #4: After they left, we ate more pie. Those who ate three pieces will remain unnamed.

Miracle #5: We needed more Stan's tire sealant for the goat heads. Jon asked about the nearest hardware store (twenty-two miles away), and the chef/owner, Larry, disappeared into the back. We discussed taking a 44-mile round-trip detour and decided against it. We didn't want to sacrifice a full day for what might turn out to be unnecessary. Jon would have to suffer the anxiety and pray for no more flats. The owner then returned with a large jug of Stan's and an injector. A previous rider had shipped it to the restaurant, didn't use it, and asked Larry to pass it on.

I am certain Jon truly manifested the Stan's. All day, as we played our usual "it's your dream" game, taking turns imagining what miracle might be waiting for us at day's end, the rest of us talked about pie. What kind, how many slices, whether we'd eat it before dinner or instead of dinner, how many pieces before we were perceived as gluttonous. But not Jon. In his state of angst, he could not imagine celebratory pie; he wanted Stan's. Tire sealant. That was his dream, a "Hail Mary" wager in the "It's your dream" game.

We assumed he was in a bit of a funk, the kind only a mechanical problem can produce. But then the universe, apparently listening with great attention to detail, delivered both: the pie we manifested for him, and the Stan's he manifested for himself. Pie Town magic at its finest.

Tonight, we're at the Pie Town RV Park. All our tires are now filled with liquid sealant, ready to battle tomorrow's goat heads. We are also filled with pie, which feels equally important.

In the campground, we met a solo woman rider, Carolyn, whose husband is following and supporting her trip with a camper. They gave us drinks. Thank you! We hope to ride together tomorrow.

Another great day—thorny, dusty, pie-filled, and full of kindness.

Chapter 11: It's Your Dream

Leaving Pie Town

Day 60 - Saturday, October 15
74.02 miles today • 2499 miles total
To Reserve, New Mexico

We packed up from the Pie Town RV Park and headed straight back to Does and Bucks for breakfast. Yes, the same place we had dinner. The pie place. Chef Larry's domain. I had a cinnamon roll (still thinking of Mimi when I eat cinnamon rolls now but happy not to share this one…), a breakfast sandwich, and two large coffees. Lois declared it the best tea on the entire Continental Divide and had two cups. We were fueled by sugar, caffeine, and optimism. We are so close to finishing, and Pie Town more than lived up to its reputation.

We dropped postcards at the post office on our way out of town and met the caretaker of the Toaster House, the local hostel. We'd chosen not to stay there after hearing a few stories, combined with our experience at the previous hostel. Sometimes discretion is the better part of adventure for avoiding nudity and butter-licking cats.

The road out of Pie Town was solid, AKA FIRM, and rideable, though you could see where it had recently been wet and muddy. The mountains ahead looked volcanic, dark, brooding, and getting closer with every mile. One of the bolts on my rack came loose and needed tightening. You learn the normal soundtrack of your bike, and any new squeak becomes a crime-scene investigation. A quick stop, a twist of the wrench, and the mystery noise was gone.

We climbed most of the morning, stopping for lunch in the sun among ponderosa pines and tiny-leafed oaks. The mountains kept inching closer. The last ten miles of trail were fast downhill, rattling us senseless on washboards. We saw a coyote and, for the first time while actually riding, an elk. We also saw an elk skin draped over a conservation sign, apparently someone's idea of commentary.

Lois dodged another snake at high speed and then a small tarantula. She's becoming quite the wildlife slalom racer, although sometimes she inadvertently takes one out. We passed two Continental Divide Trail hikers, both Japanese, and crossed another Continental Divide high point ourselves. The dancing is becoming less vigorous.

When we reached the next paved road, we saw Carolyn, the rider we'd met last night in the campground. She had just finished the section we were starting. Her husband Doug was there with the truck to pick her up. We'd hoped to ride with her today, but she must be fast. She's ridden the Divide alone, except when meeting her husband in the Airstream. I think she is brave.

With storms forecast for tomorrow, we made an alternate plan: reroute to Reserve. Forty more miles on pavement today. Two angry truck drivers passed us, even though we were already riding single file on the very edge of the road. It was the first time in sixty days we'd had truly bad interactions with vehicles, and of course they came back-to-back. It was unsettling, and I was grateful we had not had previous encounters. Mean people can be totally demoralizing, and it takes extra energy to overcome them, energy we could not spare.

Then the storm hit. Heavy rain for an hour. Heads down, legs turning, water everywhere. On pavement we rotate the lead every mile, one mile pulling, then drop to the back. The mile markers make it easy. It keeps the pace steady and gives everyone a break from the wind.

By the time we reached Reserve, it was pouring buckets. Lois vetoed the first hotel with a firm gut feeling. We regrouped in the parking lot, shivering, scrolling through our phones for something less… cowboy dangerous. We found a newer, cleaner place with no chance of bedbugs tonight. The thunder and lightning outside made us grateful for four walls and a roof.

Dinner was a change from the usual beans and rice rotation: broccoli, mashed potatoes, carrots, and tuna. A feast, relatively speaking.

We think we can finish in about five more days. It's hard to believe we've been riding for sixty days.

Counting Down the Days… and the Bag of GORP

Day 61 - Sunday, October 16
0 miles today • 2499.04 miles total
Still in Reserve, New Mexico

We awoke in Reserve, New Mexico to the kind of sky that makes you seriously consider altering your plans for the day ahead, before you've even had coffee. The plan, if you could call it that, was to decide whether to ride or not to ride. A classic trail dilemma: push on through questionable weather, or stay in a clean, warm hotel room and risk the slow death of boredom and restless legs.

We began the debate over our standard "trail breakfast," which has become redundant and eaten for fuel, not enjoyment. Today, as on most days: Starbucks instant coffee and oatmeal loaded with peanut butter. It's the kind of meal that tastes better when eaten outdoors, but we ate it indoors out of the weather, fueling our bodies and still pretending we might ride.

Eventually, reluctantly, we admitted the obvious: we were staying put. Tara and I walked into town for her coffee, and because we were in a small-town American restaurant, I felt morally obligated to order something. So, I had a second breakfast—biscuits with enough butter to violate several health guidelines, eggs, fruit, and more coffee. If you're going to be trapped by weather, you might as well carb-load.

The town itself was dreary, the kind of place where the paint gave up long before the people did. We wandered into a small shop that redeemed the entire zip code. It had everything a hiker, biker, or hunter could ever want—tire slime, dehydrated refried beans (a required staple for us and no one else), elk call whistles, jewelry, ice cream, and a general sense the owner had taken a long look at their clientele and said, "Yes. Someone will want that."

When we stepped back outside, the sky had gone from gloomy to apocalyptic. Black clouds raced overhead, and a row of crows lined up on a wire like they were auditioning for a Hitchcock movie.

They cawed at us in what I can only assume was crow for "Seek shelter, idiots."

We continued to the post office to buy a stamp, only to find it closed. It took us an embarrassingly long moment to realize it was Sunday. Trail time is not real time.

Then the heavens opened. Rain and hail hammered the pavement as we huddled under the tiny roof of an ATM, our feet getting soaked by the river forming at the curb and the splashing of the rain. When the storm eased from "biblical" to merely "unpleasant," we dashed across the road to a grocery store, bought junk food and cocoa, and retreated to the Mountaineer Motel. We drank cocoa with marshmallows in bed, peak luxury, and scratched lottery tickets Tara had purchased for entertainment. We did not win, but we congratulated ourselves on being winners in life, which is free and requires no payout.

Jon and Lois were perfectly content with a down day, and honestly, having a group to make decisions is a blessing. Tara had wanted to push on, and I would have gone with her, but it would have been miserable. We would've ended up huddled under the rain shelter, cold, wet, and questioning our judgment. Instead, we were warm, dry, and smugly vindicated. Even Tara acquiesced that staying put was the right decision.

The truth is, taking a down day is hard for both of us. Movement is our mental health. Stillness feels like a malfunction. But we made the best of it: washing mold out of water bottles, drying shoes, cleaning shorts and socks, studying the map, repairing bikes, trimming eyebrows (not mine, let's not get carried away), trimming beards (that one could be mine), and enjoying the refinement of a flush toilet.

Down days wear on the psyche. We feel like we're not making progress. We worry that if we don't move, we won't sleep, the restless legs waiting to spark to life. We know we were born to move, yet today we are confined to a small hotel room. On days like this, when staying still feels like a punishment for making a prudent decision, the miles get heavy in a different way.

I remembered another trip, when someone in our group lost their medication. Every rider immediately offered to share theirs, all four of them, except me. I wasn't taking anything for depression. And I remember wondering why I was the odd one out. Did that make me strong? Stubborn? Or simply afraid of needing help? The trail has a way of asking questions you've been avoiding for years.

Later, the four of us walked through the rain to Bill's Bar. It was… an experience. We were the only people not wearing camouflage, not hunting wild animals, and not local. The bartender and the fryer were the same person, and food was prepared one order at a time. The options were so unappealing that even we, who have eaten some truly questionable trail meals, decided to retreat to the hotel and make beans and rice. When dehydrated beans sound like the superior culinary choice, you know something is off. Part of the decision was the timing. When we need to eat, we need to eat NOW, and one fryolator meal at a time was not going to be quick enough to keep us from sliding under the table.

Speaking of food, my bag of GORP (Good Old Raisins and Peanuts) continues its daily evolution. Today's lineup included peanut butter pretzels (softening by the hour), raisins, peanuts, bridge mix, cinnamon dog biscuits, M&Ms, peanut M&Ms, fruit chews, junior mints, and circus peanuts. Just kidding, those are cinnamon cookies that only look like dog biscuits. The circus peanuts are a cozy reminder of the sugar high from childhood at my grandmother's house. She also stocked gumdrops.

We ended the day reading, restocking, calling family and friends, and feeling grateful we weren't out riding in that storm. Tomorrow, we head toward Glenwood, legs rested, spirits restored, and my GORP bag freshly mutated.

I Talk to the Cows. Really.

Day 62 - Monday, October 17
39.3 miles before the rain showers • 2538.39 miles total
To Glenwood Park Pavilion, New Mexico

I talk to cows. Every time we pass them. I can't help it. "Good mooooorning," or "Please mooooove out of the road," or whatever greeting seems appropriate for the bovine audience of the moment. They almost always respond, either with a long, thoughtful stare or an actual moo. Lois thinks I've lost it, but she also knows I never had it to begin with. I've always been odd and I am totally good with that. Tara knows it too and still chose to spend two months with me in a single tent. That's friendship, or questionable judgment, or both.

The hunters at the hotel left early, rumbling out in their big, loaded trucks at 5 a.m. We heard them debating whether they could reach their hunting grounds, since yesterday's storm had flooded the roads. Apache Creek had been underwater last night, and no one seemed entirely sure what was passable this morning.

We packed up and hit the road, grateful for the legs to be spinning again. Early in the day we climbed through a winding canyon, the landscape shifting as we moved deeper into the desert. Our first yucca plants appeared—spiky, defiant, and perfectly adapted to drought, which felt ironic given the recent weather. The downhill riding was a reward, smooth and fast, until Lois accidentally ran over a tarantula. Yikes! We were all sorry! The rivers that had been bone-dry two days ago were now roiling brown torrents, swollen with storm runoff.

We stopped in Alma at a gas station conjoined with a small restaurant, but we chose to skip a second breakfast, saving ourselves for the Glenwood Tavern near our destination. That turned out to be a tactical error: the Tavern is closed on Mondays. Who knew it was Monday? Trail time strikes again.

At the Glenwood post office, we mailed a few cards and asked the clerk about accommodations. We may be getting used to real beds; deciding if that option is "cheap enough," we will opt for a bed again. "Town" is a generous term for Glenwood, but we were hopeful. The trading post had a room, but it was out of our budget, and even more out of Jon and Lois's, given the Canadian exchange rate. Paying 1.38 times the price for the same room is a special kind of insult.

We decided to "camp" at the town park. The RV Park that did not allow tenting referred us to the local town park, which had a covered gazebo. That sounded promising, and as we rode up the one-mile hill, deer watched us pass like we were the entertainment. When we arrived, there was no "gazebo" in sight, but there was an open-sided building with picnic tables and a wooden stage. A stage. Carpeted. Dry. An irresistible draw for sleeping tonight.

Tara immediately used one of the tables for a hip-flexor stretch. Jon went to use the nature bathroom and returned with a new species of prickers attached to his pants. Prickers love Jon. They flock to him. His pants have developed a kind of fur.

Tara and I played on the swing set and the slide after the rain stopped. We are both still acting like children, which is probably why we get along so well. We rode back to the trading post for snacks to kill time before dinner. I had already eaten my planned dinner as an early afternoon snack and with no regrets. It was a delicious Thai pasta dried meal that Mimi had gifted to me.

Tara is starting to think about her new job, which begins a couple of weeks after we return home. Mimi and Larry are planning to pick us up at Antelope Wells in a rented camper, and we're hoping to give Jon and Lois a ride to the train station. We have only three or four days left. Hard to believe.

We're heading back to the park now, dollars in hand, for Jon's promised adult dance performance on the stage.

Too Much of a Good Thing? No… But Definitely a Lot of Miles for Our Butts

Day 63 - Tuesday, October 18
64.34 miles today • 2602.73 miles total
To Silver City, New Mexico

There can be too much of a good thing. Too many days on a bike seat. Too many miles. We were feeling the wear and tear of the miles, but we were happy and just complaining for the fun of it. Sixty-four miles on pavement today was enough that my butt fell off before the end of the day, somewhere around mile fifty-eight. We left it in the ditch without ceremony. Good riddance.

We'd let Jon off the hook for his promised performance last night because Tara and I had planned our own rendition of Queen's "Bicycle Race", singing, riding around the pavilion, the whole thing. It would have been terrible, but enthusiastically terrible. Unfortunately (or fortunately), we started late and it was nearly dark. I didn't see that a strap was dangling from the back end of my bike. It wrapped itself neatly into my axle and rear brake (I was thankful as I am still unable to carry a tune in a bucket) ending the performance before it began. Tara, ever the committed performer, carried on while the audience, Jon and Lois, came to my rescue and extracted the strap. They are the best companions. Tara eventually quit the performance too. We should both stick to riding our bikes.

Before bed, Lois gave us her nightly update on how many millions of hours we'd be in our sleeping bags before sunrise. Usually it's eleven or twelve hours. It sounds torturous until we lie down and realize we can't get back up.

We read that javelinas roam this area and smell similar to skunks. In the night, the pavilion smelled like skunk. I got up to pee and didn't make the connection quickly enough to scan for the creature responsible. I did my business and climbed back into the tent on the stage, blissfully unaware of what might have been watching me. We smelled the same odor a couple of times during the ride today, so I'm convinced the javelinas were out and about. Once you become attuned to that odor, it is unmistakable.

We stopped at the trading post before heading out and grabbed a couple of breakfast items. The morning was the opposite of our usual pattern: instead of clear skies turning stormy, we had clouds with big breaks of blue. We wore tights for warmth until late afternoon.

In Cliff, home to a gas station and not much else, we stopped for lunch at a picnic table in the shade. From there we could observe the tall cowboys coming and going. They all look tall because of their high-heeled boots, and the spurs were real. It was like watching a casting call for a Western, but these were "real live" cowboys, a species not found in the northeastern United States.

The morning riding was comfortable. We climbed out of Glenwood, passing rivers that were either roaring with muddy water or still completely dry. The afternoon, however, was a long, long grind. We smelled javelinas again but only saw a dead one on the road. The last 25 miles into Silver City were all uphill. Did I mention it was a long grind? It was a long grind.

We crossed another Continental Divide marker and barely had the energy for a celebration dance. The final two miles into Silver City were downhill, a mercy from the universe that I appreciated, being low on energy. We stopped at Dairy Queen, inhaled ice cream, and then mustered enough strength to go into the grocery store before heading to our fancy Motel 6 for the night.

Tomorrow, we keep inching toward the border. My butt, however, may need to be retrieved from that ditch.

Food for Thought (and More Food)

Day 64 - Wednesday, October 19
0 miles • 2602.73 miles total
Approximately 1,365,765,678 calories
Still in Silver City, New Mexico, Motel 6

Has anyone noticed I now count miles to two decimal places? I feel it is deserved, every single pedal stroke earned and accounted for.

Today was a deliberate pause, a day to let our bodies catch up to our spirits, to feel grateful for our lives and this adventure, and to refuel in Silver City, New Mexico, before the last two-day push to the Mexico border. We were also timing our arrival at the finish to match the arrival of Larry and Mimi with the camper. There wasn't much to do today except eat, wander, and appreciate the simple miracle of being here, almost 2,700 miles from where we started.

I began my refueling tour with breakfast out, and yes, I cleaned my plate. Then a quick yogurt and sparkling water back in the room. Then an ice cream snack. All before lunch. Silver City is supportive that way: food appears, and you eat it.

We found a tiny shop run by an artistic woman offering excellent cookies. Following Jon's rule, accept any and all calories from strangers, I ate one. Tara declined because of her gluten allergy, and I secretly wished to have her cookie. I thought it was too forward to ask for a second one.

Lunch was pizza and more sparkling water. Fresh water felt like a luxury these days, especially when it didn't require filtering out manure. Sparkling water felt downright decadent.

We hadn't seen Lois and Jon all day; we'd split up in the morning to run our separate errands. But the cookie lady, apparently the unofficial communications hub of Silver City, told us exactly where to find them. And she was right. We located them in a bar, drinking root beer floats and beers like two people who had also burned off their butts back around mile 2,558.

After lunch, we hit the grocery store for cookies and popcorn, an after-lunch snack, naturally, and to pick up lunches and fruit for the next two days. We ended the day at Domino's Pizza. I have worked hard today to replace the butt that fell off yesterday. It is critical if I'm going to make it to Mexico.

I did buy a new lightweight titanium spork. For the uninitiated, it is a spoon/fork combination utensil. It feels like a responsible investment in my future. I have a plastic one, but I've already broken one of those, and the spork has become the most critical piece of gear when you are burning thousands of calories a day. Forget carbon frames and GPS units, give me a utensil that won't snap under pressure.

Silver City itself is full of murals and desert color. The guys at the bike shop were kind enough to loosen my pedals in preparation for the upcoming packing of my bike for the flight home. Small kindnesses feel enormous out here and removing pedals before packing the bikes is one of those notoriously difficult tasks after a long ride.

I have a good life and great friends, both old and new. And I'm starting to think about returning home to John and my family. Very grateful.

Larry and Mimi will meet us tomorrow night to share our last day and our arrival into Antelope Wells, New Mexico, on the U.S.–Mexico border. Tomorrow's ride is half dirt, half pavement. Sunshine is in the forecast. We all have mixed emotions as this great adventure begins its final descent.

Chapter 12: Finishing the Ride, Starting the Reckoning

The Long Road Home

Going home is sometimes harder than being away. On the road, I miss John, and on the phone, we sound like our best selves—easy, familiar, stitched together by nearly four decades of shared language. But in person, something shifts. We move around each other like riders who know the route but have fallen out of sync with the cadence. After thirty-seven years, connection isn't automatic; it's something we have to find again each time.

Part of the distance comes from the world we live in now. Our beliefs have drifted, tugged apart by the currents of our separate social media streams. It's a quiet divide, but a real one, widening in ways neither of us intended. We don't argue about it; we just feel the space it creates.

Part of it is aging. I wake at 1:30 every night now, as if my body has forgotten the second half of sleep. Our biorhythms have always been mismatched — his whole family is made of night owls; mine practically race the sunrise. And then there's the hearing. He does his best with two hearing aids, but they can only do so much against the slow creep of auditory loss. Half our conversations now involve me repeating myself, him taking a wild guess, and both of us laughing because neither of us is entirely sure what was actually said.

Marriage really is a team sport. We're two people who once slept without thinking about it, now tag-teaming the slightly slapstick betrayals of time — one early riser, one night owl, each of us grateful for the personal space those differences create. What we share now is a whole lot of patience, and the sense that we're navigating all of this together, even when we're awake at completely different hours.

And part of it is the simple truth that long marriages evolve. They stretch, contract, fray, mend. In the car from the airport, I felt a tightness in my chest—not pain exactly, but a pressure that felt like worry. I told myself my life is easy, that I have nothing to complain about. But beneath that reassurance was a quieter fear: what if content is not good enough?

Still, this is the life we built. Not perfect, not effortless, but reassuring. A long marriage isn't defined by constant closeness; it's defined by the willingness to stay when closeness ebbs. We have weathered moves, careers, illnesses, losses, and the slow drift of time. We have rituals that anchor us, history that holds us, and a kind of loyalty that doesn't need to be loud to be real.

Sometimes I think of our marriage the way I think of a long trip, one of those multi-week rides where the terrain keeps changing and you don't always like the section you're in. Some days are smooth and companionable, the miles passing easily. Some days you ride in silence, not because anything is wrong, but because you're each managing your own effort. And some days you're out of rhythm entirely, climbing at different speeds, stopping at different times, wondering why the other person can't just match your pace.

But you keep moving forward because the journey matters more than any single stretch of road. You trust that the trail will shift again, that the hard miles aren't the whole story, and that the person riding beside you is still the one you chose—just older now, just human, just trying.

Maybe that's what commitment looks like after nearly four decades: not a seamless connection, but a durable one. Not the absence of distance, but the choice to bridge it repeatedly. Not a guarantee of happiness, but a shared life that still matters, even when the terrain gets rough.

And maybe that's why the Divide felt so familiar—another long road, another test of endurance, another reminder that the hard miles are part of the story.

On Top of the World with Only One Day Left

Day 65 - Thursday October 20
80 miles today • 2,683.6 miles total
To Hachita, New Mexico

We rolled our bikes down the hallway of the Motel 6 like rats scurrying from a hole, hoping not to be seen. For our $52 room, Lois appointed herself the "maintenance man" of the rat hole, cleaning drains and unclogging the toilet to make the room functional. She's one of the most self-sufficient people I know—direct, determined, unflappable. A classic accounting personality: everything black and white, factual, no nonsense. Exactly the kind of person you want on an adventure.

We stopped at the Javelina Café for coffee, a spot our friend Bob had recommended. With a name like that, how could we not? It did not smell like a javelina, but of hot coffee and pastries. We were still hoping to manifest an actual javelina, since we hadn't seen a live one yet, though we had become very familiar with their unique scent.

Leaving Silver City, we made a slight navigational error and ended up below the road we needed. At this stage, adding miles was unacceptable. So, we bushwhacked straight up the steep bank, pushing our loaded bikes through thorny brush. By the time we reached the road, we were covered in prickers. They were embedded in clothing, skin, everywhere. Jon now resembled a hedgehog, and I've decided he enjoys that look. We spent a few minutes plucking them out. Some problems demand immediate attention as ignoring them only makes them worse.

The first few miles were uphill on tarmac. We chatted with a few members of the Silver City Bike Club when they overtook us, many of them women, all of them spiffily dressed. Where we were pure function, they were fit and fashionable. I have never been accused of being fashionable.

Then came the descent: long, smooth, glorious. We turned onto dirt for the rest of the day, just as planned. The gravel was in good shape, and we passed a horned bull, a donkey, and plenty of cows. I'm still talking to them.

Good moooorning! Nice day today! We're almost done! Have a great day.

The song looping in my head was "Top of the World," and that is exactly how I felt. Over and over. I'm on top of the world, overflowing with joie de vivre.

We reached the Separ Trading Post—a dusty gravel lot, a weathered wooden building, historic and ridiculously expensive. As the only service stop for miles, it was a full-blown tourist trap. We didn't care. We bought ice cream and snacks anyway, not that there were any other options. A border patrol agent with a horse trailer was parked outside. As he drove off, his insulated coffee mug tumbled into the lot, but he was gone before we could return it.

We decided to push another twenty-seven miles to Hachita. The first seven miles were on a wash boarded frontage road. Sadly, our last dirt stretch was also one of the worst, pounding both ends of the spectrum: our wrists and our nether regions. Tara would have some serious nerve damage in her hands as a result, but I can't speak for her nether region. Then came twenty miles on what might be the quietest paved road in America. Only a couple of vehicles passed us, the now ubiquitous FedEx trucks and border patrol.

In Hachita, we followed our trail notes and stopped at the small general store for the key to the community center. Two border patrol agents were there too, with horses and very large guns. The person behind the counter handed over the key without hesitation. The community center was just up the road and inside were the accommodations weary riders needed: food, cots, a flush toilet, and space. Some of the food was outdated, some soggy, some edible—we know because we sampled much of it. There was even a stage practically begging for a performance.

While I was outside talking to (my) John on the phone, a man in a dilapidated truck pulled up to the curb. As he leaned forward, I saw a big knife tucked into the back of his pants. He offered us fresh carrots, peppers, and squash, said nothing else, and drove off. Tara and I looked at each other, shrugged, ate the carrots, and planned to cook the peppers. We assumed he worked on a local farm and had plenty to spare. The generosity of a local farmer was always appreciated. As we approached the end of this adventure, just as on the day we started, we were the recipients of unexpected kindness.

There are many good people out here. We anxiously waited for Mimi and Larry to arrive in the rented camper.

> As the Divide wound toward its end, that familiar mix of pride and melancholy settled in, the heaviness that comes when a long adventure begins to taper. My body was tired, my mind stretched thin, and the remaining miles felt both too few and, with one day left, still a challenge. The finish was close enough to imagine, but not close enough to touch. That in-between place has its own gravity.
>
> It reminded me of the days after Ironman Arizona. Not the race itself, but the quiet that followed, when the adrenaline drained and the meaning of it all began to take shape. After I returned home, I wavered between inspiration and melancholy. Fall always brings a heaviness. I want to keep doing wild adventures, to test myself, but I am tired. And then I think of Leigh, a cancer survivor, now an Ironman, and I wonder what right I have to use age or fatigue as a reason to shrink my world in my "go-go" years. I will continue to use Leigh as my inspiration.
>
> She had not only persevered through a medical challenge but then went on to complete a race that fewer than 0.01% of the population has done. The full Ironman one of the rarest athletic accomplishments on Earth.

Out on the Divide, in those final miles, I felt the first stirrings of a transformation I wouldn't fully grasp until much later—after watching Leigh become an Ironman, after realizing how endurance reshapes you quietly, from the inside out. You don't always notice it happening. One day you just look up and realize you're different than when you started.

Maybe that's the real finish line, not the border crossing or the last mile, but the moment you understand what the journey has made of you. And maybe that's true of marriage too. You don't always see the change as it's happening. You just look up one day and realize you've both been reshaped by the miles you've traveled together.

WE DID IT!

Day 66 - Friday October 21
45.39 miles today • 2,728.12 miles total
To Antelope Wells, New Mexico

Larry and Mimi arrived last night in a rented camper, and Larry made omelets for dinner in the community house in Hachita, which allows bikers to stay inside. We were all elated and simultaneously subdued as we cooked, each of us privately contemplating the end of this adventure. Mimi, Larry, Tara, and I slept in the camper parked beside the building, while Jon and Lois slept on cots inside.

We had fresh fruit and yogurt for breakfast, thanks to our camper friends. We packed our bikes for the final time, said our temporary goodbyes, and headed out just after 7:30 a.m., hoping to outrun the wind that was guaranteed to arrive later. The ride was completely flat, the pavement smooth, and the desert offered up its usual oddities: two toilets and a chair abandoned in the sand, four flattened rattlesnakes, and two live ones sunbathing directly on the road. Road signs promised buffalo, but despite our attempts at manifesting them, none appeared. We did, however, pass one dead, impressively odiferous coyote. My passing thought: that could have been me in the ditch, a desiccated shell after attempting a challenge this bold for someone pushing sixty. I not only survived, but the four of us were going to make it to the finish, stronger than when we began.

With twenty-one miles to go, Mimi and Larry drove past in the camper, cheering with huge smiles. Mimi rang her cowbell with the enthusiasm of a one-woman parade. Border Patrol vehicles passed regularly, some towing horse trailers or four-wheelers. Tara even lay down in the middle of the road, a bold move for her, to prove as we'd read, that it *was* the least-driven paved road in America. Fortunately, she is still alive, and she proved the point. I think that move reflects how much she has grown during this adventure too.

We stopped for lunch on the roadside, eating snacks in warm but pleasant weather. The wind picked up but never turned hostile. I felt strong and appreciated the flat terrain. My elation from yesterday wasn't present; perhaps the foreboding of life returning to normal was settling in.

Lois seemed to be flagging, her lack of energy foreshadowing a serious health challenge she would face a couple of months later. They would finish this portion of their year-long adventure but cut the Baja and Mexico ride short due to COVID and, ultimately, a cancer diagnosis.

A helicopter flew overhead, and soon we could see a long, unnatural line on the horizon. As we drew closer, it sharpened into the border wall, far more imposing than anything I had imagined. Tall, endless, its vertical bars looked like a giant jail cell stretching in both directions. As we approached the final yards near the border security building, Mimi and Larry were waiting, Mimi ringing her cowbells in full celebration.

The four of us had a photo session and stripped down our bikes so we could lift them for the traditional finishing photo. With all the gear removed, we each raised our bikes overhead, proof of what we had done. Then took turns photographing ourselves in various configurations: Jon and Lois; Larry and Tara; and Tara, Mimi, and me.

Wow. We did it. We rode over 2,700 miles. From Canada to the Mexico border. We rode the Great Divide Mountain Bike Route.

Typical of our group, there was no extended celebration. We simply moved on to the next task in the orderly, efficient way we'd developed over two months of traveling together. We packed and organized everything for the drive west to Tucson. It took a while. Six people and four bikes required puzzle-level creativity, but eventually we closed the camper doors and headed out, riding in a vehicle for only the second time in over ten weeks.

It hasn't really sunk in that we did it. Women pushing sixty can still outride their doubts, carrying more years than most riders out here and still crossing a continent. We were thrilled Mimi made it to the finish to celebrate with us, and we hope to ride it again with her someday.

We stopped at Dairy Queen and camped at Crazy Horse, an odd little campground on the outskirts of Tucson. Larry and Mimi made a great dinner, which we ate outside in the warm evening air.

Over dinner I asked, "Tara, would you do it again?"

No hesitation.

"Yeah! But on a mountain bike!"

The Days After
How much life do I have left

After arriving home, a friend organized a small "welcome home" gathering, and there was a brief write-up in the local newspaper. Quickly, though, life settled back into its familiar rhythm—yardwork, family, running, and planning the next adventure. I did reflect on the trip, my personal growth, and a renewed commitment to living my dreams.

More recently, I revisited the math of my remaining years. I like math—or at least I thought I did—until I attempted to read *Euclid in the Rainforest: Discovering Universal Truth in Logic and Math* by Joseph Mazur. I love to read, and I love math, but this book is operating several floors above my current mental capacity. Perhaps it's because I retired, and along with the stress and meetings, my brain retired too. It's probably lounging somewhere, resting, having completed nine sudoku puzzles, and occasionally rechecking the house square footage for the new insurance policy.

Anyway, my life math is simple. If my retirement plan actuary is accurate, I will live to be ninety-four. My birthday is in January, so using January first as the start date and assuming death at ninety-four, I had thirty-eight years remaining when I quit working. That meant I still had forty percent of my total estimated days on Earth to achieve my dreams. I had 13,870 days left—332,880 hours. Big numbers. At the time, they seemed enormous. Now, at sixty-one, they seem… slightly less enormous, and a good reminder to stay focused on those dreams.

Five years into retirement, I've used up thirteen percent of my "retirement time." Do the math for yourself. If your actuarial table is accurate, do you still have time to "live your dreams." I'm confident that quitting at an "early retirement" age allowed me to achieve some of mine—dreams that waiting until sixty-seven would have quietly smothered. The first 1,825 days were invested wisely: I accomplished enormous life goals, survived a broken nose, and even a chainsaw accident involving my left pinky finger. Not exactly the conventional path to enlightenment, but certainly memorable, humbling, and character-building.

Now I have thirty-three years—12,045 days—remaining. Whoa. Enough time to feel urgent, yet long enough to laugh at the idea that retirement is a slow, gentle cruise. At the speed I've been achieving things, like writing this book, I do occasionally worry that it might not be completed before my illustrious expiration date in 2059. But that's okay. Some dreams don't unfold the way you envision. My first 1,825 days of retirement weren't "used up." They were invested.

Writing isn't a race against death; it's a compression algorithm for life. A page takes hours, but meaning is measured in lived experience. And honestly, the fear that the book won't be finished is minimal compared to worrying about my husband and the possibility of losing the man who plows the driveway, loves the cat, and makes the necessary trips to the dump. Those worries are singular unto me.

Retirement didn't retire my brain. It simply removed deadlines and added perspective. Euclid didn't get harder because I got weaker. It got harder because I now prefer meaning over proof. That's evolution, not decline.

If there's one recalculation I'd offer, it's this: don't measure the remaining days by how much you can do. Measure them by how much you can truly experience the life you were meant to live.

And by that metric, I'm doing just fine. Even if my pinky finger occasionally disagrees.

So here's the conclusion, prior to the next documented adventure: life is messy, retirement is mathy, and writing is difficult for an engineer—and yet, glorious chaos. Perhaps my three-year delay in completion was simply so AI could evolve enough to assist in my pitiful efforts. I followed my dream and learned a few things—about numbers, about dreams, and about the surprising arithmetic of living.

An author friend recently said, "No book is ever truly finished." I learned early in project management that sometimes you have to shoot the engineer and get on with the project. So, believing that a book is never finished, it just gets published, here it is. As good as it's going to be. Like a mentor once told the perfectionist: "Eighty percent is good enough." It pissed me off. But now, it feels okay—good enough to check "write a book" off my list, balanced by the 120 percent I'm giving to my life.

The book may or may not be truly finished, but the laughter, the scratches, the broken bones, the adventures, and the stories will carry over to a sequel. Hopefully before I die at ninety-four.

The pages end here, but the trail doesn't. Sixty-six days on a bike while approaching sixty years old showed me that the best parts of life aren't behind me—they're waiting just up the road.

Retiring was the right thing. We have enough.

Author's Note

I set out to write a book about a bike trip. That was the whole plan: document the miles, the mishaps, the cows, the prickers, the climbs, the people, the weather, the grit. A straightforward account of a long ride down the spine of a continent.

Along the way, the story widened. The trail had a way of shaking loose memories, questions, old versions of myself, and the quiet truths I'd tucked into the corners of my life. The miles didn't just move me south; they moved me inward. And suddenly the book wasn't just about the Divide anymore. It was about the life I carried onto it.

So, the life stories came in. Not because I planned them, but because they insisted on being part of the journey. The trip gave them context; the memories gave the trip meaning. Together, they told a fuller truth than either could on its own.

If you've made it to this page, thank you for riding with me, through the dust, the doubt, the laughter, the math, the marriage, the aging body, the stubborn mind, and the long stretches of road where nothing happened except the slow, steady work of becoming someone braver than you were the day before.

I wrote this book the same way I rode the Divide: one section at a time, occasionally lost, occasionally cursing, occasionally wondering why I ever thought this was a good idea. But also, with joy. And awe. And the deep gratitude that comes from realizing you're still capable of more than you imagined.

If there's anything I hope you take from these pages, it's this: adventure doesn't have an age limit. Reinvention doesn't expire. And the best parts of life don't live behind you, they wait ahead, disguised as ordinary days, unplanned detours, and bold decisions you're not entirely sure you're ready for.

The trail doesn't end at the border. Mine didn't, and yours won't either. There are more miles ahead, some smooth, some wash boarded, some that will make you question your sanity. Ride them anyway. Lift your bike overhead when you can. Eat the ice cream. Talk to the cows. Laugh at the math. And when in doubt, remember, eighty percent is good enough.

A final thanks you to everyone who helped shape it, edit it, rearrange it—Mom, Angela, Jessica, Val, Barb, Paula, Mary, Monica and everyone I have not listed! It is better from your efforts. And thank you to my audience and those who followed my adventure. I truly hope it nudges you toward your own.

Jenny

Biography

Jenny Cusick holds a degree in Chemical Engineering and an MBA, which she applied over a long career in manufacturing before choosing to spend her time in the places that had always mattered most to her: the mountains, the trails, and the open water.

A lifelong runner, she has completed numerous marathons, an ultramarathon, and a wide range of endurance activities. She spent nearly a decade as a wilderness EMT, volunteer, and board member with the Pemigewasset Valley Search and Rescue Team in northern New Hampshire, supporting people in crisis while deepening her own connection to the backcountry.

Her hiking background includes the Appalachian Trail through Maine, New Hampshire, and Vermont; all of New Hampshire's 4,000-foot peaks; and Mount Katahdin's Knife Edge. She later earned her Maine Guide Sea Kayak License and now spends many days exploring the Maine coast by paddle.

Since retiring, Jenny has continued to pursue long-distance travel and outdoor expeditions, including bikepacking routes from Canada to Mexico, across British Columbia, and throughout the United States. She values the clarity, humility, and camaraderie that come from moving through the world under her own power.

Through her writing she hopes to encourage others, especially those entering the second half of life, to trust their curiosity, step toward the unfamiliar, and discover what adventure can offer when approached with preparation, humor, and an open mind.

Made in the USA
Coppell, TX
30 June 2026

83235633R00134